THE LIFE OF TAPA

My Journey
with a Blue Heeler

and a Guide
to Happier, Healthier D

For the love of our dogs,
Annie Horkan

Annie Horkan

The Life of Tapa

First Printing February 2014

Red Bear Press
192 Main Street, Suite 8
Ellsworth, Maine 04634

ISBN 978-0-9896153-9-6

Book Design:
Birdwalk Studio
Blue Hill, Maine

Printed in the USA

In Memory of Tapa

I had been through
the heartbreak
and loss of the canine
loyal love before.

Five years had passed
when I finally opened my
heart to let this love
seep in again.

You came to me
on a warm September evening
in the shadows of the Blue Ridge,
unexpectedly.

How could I have doubted
then, what would become
one of the deepest bonds
never to be broken.
You hid beneath the chairs
for days until my long
outstretched hand on your belly
beckoned closer rubs.

Those sweet belly rubs
sealed the deal...and
we went forth forever
bound at the hip and the heart.

From the rolling green fields
of Appalachian beauty
to the enchanted high desert
we moved.

With long hikes amidst towering Ponderosa,
through meandering arroyos and mystical canyons,
and along the Mexican ocean's edge
we played.

You never complained, whined,
argued, doubted or retreated.
You accepted, smiled, believed,
trusted and defended.
These are not words to tell
yet another story.
These are words about
a dog who touched a heart.

My heart,
a broken heart,
a forgotten heart,
was found.

You have shown me
in your dying
the truth in living.

*I know now why dog
is god spelled backwards…
your heart is full of
perfect love.*

*These are words about
the brave heart,
who keeps loving
in the face of death.*

*You would stay if I let you,
and battle to the end.
I will not allow this tropical fate
to have its way with you.
You deserve to go out with dignity
for all you gave me…
silently, peacefully, slip into
the warm embrace of the turquoise sea.*

*In the quiet
of the house
I will feel
the whispers of your spirit.*

*I will go on,
holding on,
to when we meet again
on the beautiful rainbow bridge.*

Contents

Contents – continued

Contents - continued

HumaneSociety.org

Ten percent of all book sales from *The Life of Tapa* will be donated to the Humane Society to support all the amazing work they do for the protection and celebration of animals throughout the world. You can read more about them below.

"The Humane Society of the United States is the nation's largest animal protection organization, rated the most effective by its peers. Since 1954, The HSUS has been fighting for the protection of all animals through advocacy, education, and hands-on programs. We rescue and care for tens of thousands of animals each year, but our primary mission is to prevent cruelty before it occurs. We're there for all animals, across America and around the world.

The HSUS seeks a humane and sustainable world for all animals—a world that will also benefit people. We are America's mainstream force against cruelty, exploitation and neglect, as well as the most trusted voice extolling the human-animal bond.

We work to reduce suffering and to create meaningful social change for animals by advocating for sensible public policies, investigating cruelty and working to enforce existing laws, educating the public about animal issues, joining with corporations on behalf of animal-friendly policies, and conducting hands-on programs that make ours a more humane world. We are a leading disaster relief agency for animals, and we provide direct care for thousands of animals at our sanctuaries and rescue facilities, wildlife rehabilitation centers, and mobile veterinary clinics.

We celebrate pets, as well as wildlife and habitat protection. We are the nation's most important advocate for local humane societies, providing shelter standards and evaluations, training programs, a national advertising campaign to promote pet adoption, direct support, and national conferences. We operate a Humane Wildlife Services program in the D.C. metro area to provide homeowners and businesses with humane and effective solutions to conflicts with our wild neighbors. We promote scientific innovation by driving the development of humane alternatives to replace harmful animal experiments. The HSUS publishes All Animals, a membership magazine, and Animal Sheltering, a bi-monthly magazine for animal sheltering professionals.

We confront national and global cruelties through major campaigns targeting the barbaric practices of dog fighting and cock fighting; abusive puppy mills where dogs are treated not like family but like production machines; the worst cruelties of factory farming in modern agribusiness, such as confinement of animals in crates and cages; inhumane and unsporting hunting practices such as "canned hunts" of captive exotic animals; the suffering of animals in experimentation, including chimpanzees and pets; the slaughter of American horses for export to foreign countries where horse meat is considered a delicacy; and the clubbing of baby seals and other animals for the commercial fur trade. Our track record of effectiveness has led to meaningful victories for animals in Congress, state legislatures, courtrooms and corporate boardrooms."

Acknowledgements

I would first like to thank those whose professional lives are dedicated to the health and care of our beloved pets.

I thank Dr. Spencer Goldstein at Biscayne Animal Hospital here in North Miami for his gentle demeanor, kind heart, his open mind to homeopathy and alternative treatments and all his genuine efforts to help save my dog. Tapa won his heart like she did so many and I know he wished the outcome of his efforts had been different.

I thank Dr. Johanna Buster at Biscayne Animal Hospital for her knowledge of Leptospirosis, and her intuitive suspicion to start Tapa on treatment for it before it was diagnosed.

I think Diana Moon Hayes of Holistic Animal Medicines in Australia for being a conscious woman with the courage to embrace higher wisdom, and to pioneer an alternative path in animal care. The world needs more vets like her.

Secondly, I would like to thank my family and friends for all their loving support through the sad and challenging time of Tapa's illness and loss.

I thank my mother, Eve Pope, for her love and financial support during this time when she was also faced with the choice to put down her sweet Corgi after many years of loyal companionship.

I thank my son, Joshua Ryan, for his love and financial support in the face of losing Tapa, whose brother, Chile, is his sweet Blue Heeler companion.

I thank my son, James Ryan, for his loving kindness and financial support. He took many hours out of his working days to help me administer fluids, run errands and stayed by my side until the bitter end. I thank his lovely wife, Fina Ryan, for her many efforts, kindness and compassion.

I thank my dear friend, Rosario Carelli, whose visit during Tapa's illness provided comfort to both Tapa and myself in countless ways, and for his keen insights and editing skills.

I thank my friend, Eva Arroyo, whose dependable friendship provided me with hope, encouragement and compassion from her consistent calls and visits.

Lastly, I thank my brother, Tony Horkan, whose willingness to invest in this book has touched me deeply.

Above all, I thank my long-time friend, Jonathon Ray Spinney, whose faith in me and my writing skills provided the opportunity for this book to be published. Thanks to all those at Red Bear Press whose work made this book possible.

Introduction

On Friday August 9, 2013, I put my sweet Blue Heeler named Tapa down for an eternal sleep. She had just turned eight years old. It was the saddest day of my life.

I am compelled to write about this long, hard journey of the last five months with her because I learned so much about dogs, about caring for them and about myself. I would like to pay it forward with this information and wisdom in the hope it will help other dog owners who not only may be challenged by the perils of canine kidney disease and failure, but who want to provide their dogs with the absolute best care. Though some of my focus will be directed to Blue Heeler dogs in particular, what I share here is by no means limited to just this breed. Every dog owner will be able to extract and gain valuable understanding from within these pages.

We are living today in a complex world which saturates and bombards us daily with information overload. As dog owners, we place our faith in the experts out there who provide guidance and assistance in the form of medical treatment, training and products for our beloved dogs. We trust that when our dog is sick, traditional veterinary medicine will provide a cure; we trust that when our dog is displaying unacceptable behavior, a professional dog trainer will have the answer; we trust the pet superstores are providing us with the best food and products to care for our dogs. Yet, veterinary medicine is riddled with the dangers of vaccines and drugs much like human allopathic medicine; professional dog training is not always successful; and the pet superstores are full of unhealthy, toxic products much like our human supermarkets. As much as we would like to trust and depend upon what is being offered, this may not always be a wise choice.

Gone are the days of simply choosing between dog food brands A or B or following the local vet's advice on your dog's health issues. There are so many dog food brands on the market today, it makes your head spin. Veterinary clinics are everywhere, and busier than ever before treating dogs for all kinds of new ailments at exorbitant prices. The rising expenses for veterinary treatment now demand dog owners to carry pet insurance. Our busy, modern lifestyle, designed to keep us working more so we can buy more, results in many dogs being cooped up at home for ten hours or more a day. Our natural environments are becoming increasingly toxic. Urban environments create dog restrictions in natural areas and parks resulting in the limitations of dog parks as the only option for you and your dog to enjoy nature.

Though we have domesticated our dogs to the max, they are still wild at heart. If our dogs could talk to us, they might tells us how much they dislike the food we feed them, how sad they are to be left home alone all day, how unnatural dog parks are and how badly vaccines and drugs make them feel. Though intuitively we may know all this, we cannot provide the best care for our dogs unless we learn to listen to them. They are talking to us. We need to watch and learn. It requires some effort, time and adjustments on our part. It is so worth it. Most good dog trainers will tell us we need to learn to listen to our dogs first before we expect them to listen to us. Thus, the place we find both the problems and solutions for our dog's unwanted behavior is usually within ourselves.

Tapa was a very healthy dog before she became sick. It was not in her living, but in her dying, that I learned to really listen to her. In retrospect, I see where and how she was trying to tell me things to which I was not listening. Dogs vibrate to the Alpha brain wave frequency. Humans only vibrate in Alpha frequency when we get quiet, relax, meditate or prior to sleep. Most of the time we are fully engaged in Beta brain wave frequencies to which our dogs do not relate. Miraculous things can happen in the connection with our dog when we slow down and allow our brains to operate in Alpha mode. My whole life came to a halt to care for her illness, and as a result, my connection to Tapa grew in ways I never thought possible with a dog. She taught me in her illness how to sit quietly with her, to put my own sorrow and stress aside and to commune with her. Though I was not always sure about what she needed, or was feeling, the effort alone carried us both to new depths.

Blue Heeler dogs are quite special, and I elaborate more on these amazing Australian cattle dogs as a breed in Chapter 2. They are extremely tough dogs, yet amazingly sensitive and sweet. They are exceptionally loyal and smart. This breed has been mixed with the wild Australian dingo dog, and as such, Heelers have a strong wild streak compared to other domesticated and over-bred dogs. Perhaps for this reason, and others of which I am not aware, Heelers do not tolerate vet meds and drugs as well as other breeds. My experience has taught me that you can offer your Heeler better medical care with homeopathy rather than traditional veterinary medicine.

We live in a toxic world in which both humans and dogs are ever more susceptible to strains of new viruses and bacteria as well as more pollutants in our environment. We need to be looking out for our dogs as much as ourselves which includes preventive and homeopathic medicine, vitamins, herbs, healthy oils, food and water. Most traditional veterinarians will not offer this kind of information. It is important to know there are many options available to help you maintain the optimal health and happiness of your dog.

Please note that I am not a veterinarian. The advice I offer you in this book is based on my personal experience in the care of my dog with her personal health issues that may not apply to your dog's health situation. I strongly recommend you always seek professional advice before adjusting any health protocols to suit your own dog. The suggestions I make are the result of my extensive research in the areas of veterinary medicine and homeopathy for which I share my personal experience and knowledge gained. This experience and knowledge is not intended to replace professional advice nor the use of your own discretion in the care of your dog. The information provided here is designed to offer you new concepts and alternatives in dog care for which you can apply to your own dog as you deem valuable and helpful.

In this book I will share with you what I have learned about:

- The connection between God and dog

- The purpose of your dog's companionship role in your life

- Adventures from loving and living with a down under dog

- Caring for a sick dog

- Leptospirosis as a deadly, aggressive bacteria that is on the rise

- The good and the bad of traditional veterinary medicine

- Homeopathy as an excellent alternative to vet meds

- Preventive care to keep your dog strong and healthy

- The ideal dog diet

- Homemade recipes you can easily make as an alternative to buying dog food

- Death as being a mysterious transformation which has no end

- The love of a dog

- My capacity to love

It has been three weeks today since sweet Tapa drifted silently to the other side. I still cry and my heart still hurts. Her ashes are placed in a beautiful, cobalt blue glass and silver urn. I find myself moving the urn into whichever room I am in just so I can be near her. It is my sincere hope by writing and sharing this information, I will pay forward a gift to help you on your journey with whatever breed of wonderful dog you may have in your life. And perhaps my heart will heal, as I let go of my dog Tapa—my best friend, companion, and primal teacher I ever had.

Though I long deeply every day to see her smiling face and relish in the joy she brought to me, it was in her dying departure that she gave me the greatest gift of all: the key to my own heart, in which I am uncovering the role of my own true purpose in living.

In Tapa's memory,

Annie Horkan
August 30, 2013

God and Dog

There is a legend which tells the story of God giving names to all his creations while strolling among them. God is said to have been followed all this time by a creature for whom he saved the best name for last: Dog—his own name spelled backwards. I do not think God would have done so unless dog was so completely deserving of having his creator's name embedded in his. There is simply no other creature on earth who exemplifies the absolute unconditional love for another as a dog. In God and in dog we find the mystery of love. No matter how many times we may be knocked down by some of life's hard lessons, we pull ourselves up and try again. We have faith everything in life happens for a reason, that our beloved creator will help us forgive ourselves and others for our mistakes and be our guide to something better. Our beloved dogs, no matter how neglected, misunderstood, abused or abandoned, will continue to shower us with their loving smiles, nudges and wagging tails. While we humans struggle to love someone who has hurt us, our dogs are an endless streaming rainbow of pure love. There is nothing we can do to lose the love of our dog. Dogs are the masters of love, a Divine gift to us to teach us the depths and wonders of unconditional loving.

❤

When God had made the earth and sky,
the flowers and the trees.
He then made all the animals,
The fish, the birds and bees.

And when at last He'd finished,

Not one was quite the same.

He said, "I'll walk this world of mine,

And give each one a name."

And so He traveled far and wide

And everywhere He went,

A little creature followed Him

Until its strength was spent.

When all were named upon the earth

And in the sky and sea,

The little creature said, "Dear Lord,

There's not one left for me."

Kindly the Father said to him,

"I've left you to the end.

I've turned my own name back to front

And called you dog, my friend."

— *Author Unknown*

Since love is so connected to the emotions, it spurs the question as to the emotional capacity of dogs, as well as their ability to have feelings. Though many people may be quick to dismiss a dog's ability to feel, there are far too many amazing animal stories which prove this ability. I recently read a story about a man in

Africa who had spent most of his life caring for and protecting elephants. Within days of his death, many miles away from the elephant herds, the elephants appeared outside his house. They could obviously feel his departure, and came to pay tribute to him. As well, there are many incredible stories of dogs whose actions irrefutably demonstrate this capability to feel. I witness in dogs their ability to feel an intense and pure love untainted by all the complexity and ambiguity of human love. We humans are endlessly consumed with the polarity struggle of love and hate, or indifference, which sabotages our quest for the higher love for which dogs have clearly been gifted. I would have been shocked by any sense of Tapa demonstrating indifference in my direction. Rather, she was a live spark of continuous and present loving energy, an eternal flame which burned its way into the depths of my heart and forever left its mark.

It is curious how dog owners can resemble their dogs, and dogs can take on certain characteristics of their owners. As this can also be found amongst human companions, it indicates the depth of bonding which occurs between a dog and their owner. Most dog owners possess the human tendency to project their traits, desires and expectations onto their dog. One can learn much about a person by meeting their dog. Many of the unacceptable and undesirable behaviors found in dogs are simply the result of their owner's conscious or unconscious projections onto them. Dogs are keen observers and eager to please. Thus, they will tend to learn behaviors as a result of these projections. It behooves us instead to watch and learn from our dogs as the masters of love, and allow their wisdom to guide us in becoming loving masters. Our dogs give us what other humans rarely give us. A dog will crack your heart wide open when you realize no matter how many mistakes you make, you will never be criticized, judged nor condemned by your dog. In this alone, our dogs elevate us to a greater capacity of understanding the love we long for. We need our dogs, and they need us.

The fact that dogs cannot verbally communicate with us is exactly how they pull us into the mystery of life and love. Sometimes when I would find myself off track energetically, Tapa would give me this deep penetrating gaze. I would usually gaze back just as intensely, and then say, "*What?*" But I knew what this expression was. I did not need to hear a single word to know it. Just her look said it all. We humans can learn from this. How quick we are to add the stinging words behind our looks when just the look is sufficient. Perhaps that is why dogs do not talk our language... to teach us a better way. For when we silence the ego's relentless needs and move instead into the heart's compassion, we find there is no need for words that sting. We remember in our silence the love we are here to give. We cannot hear the voice of God while we are busy entertaining and being distracted by the ego's dramas. It is in the silence that both God and our dog speak to us.

Abraham Lincoln was noted as saying, *"I care not for a man's religion whose dog and cat are not the better for it."* I find it interesting a man of such stature would so humbly acknowledge our pets as significant of Divine reflection. But then, he was the humanitarian who saw the need to end slavery. And he must have had a dog. He would then have understood how dogs give us their unshakable loyalty and forgiveness as a friend and guide beyond the limitations of man. Our dogs gift us with not only a dependable, meaningful relationship beyond many of our human relationships, but bestow upon us their wise, soulful looks, their soothing presence, their capacity to transform our sorrow and provide a listening ear without interruption. They fill our days with boundless joy and gratitude, while blessing us with a drama free existence. At the end of the day, we come to understand through our canine companion's reflection just how well we are capable of loving ourselves and others. Along with God, our dog grants us the grace-filled insight into how to love unconditionally.

I once dated a man who did not like dogs. A few months into our relationship, my wonderful yellow Labrador, Timber, was hit by a car. The little neighbor girls on the hill would often come down to play ball with Timber, and they were told never to throw the ball if the gate was open. But I guess in their childish innocence and eager desire to play with her, they overlooked the open gate, and Timber ended up in the road in pursuit of the ball. It was a hit and run. An elderly woman driving behind the car that hit her stopped, wrapped her in a blanket and called me. Timber had been laying in the shade in the yard just ten minutes earlier. She died early the next morning. My boyfriend and I were scheduled to go out of town the next day, which we did after I buried my dog. I was devastated, and could not stop crying. I was grieving, which is what we are supposed to do. My boyfriend got tired of my tears and finally looked at me and said, *"When are you going to stop crying? It was just a dog."* I knew right then our relationship would never last. I told him in response that I felt sorry for him.

People who never have a dog do not know what they are missing. I realize not everyone's life circumstances allow for having a dog nor do some people want the responsibility. While my friends who do not have dogs liked and enjoyed my dog, they also found my love for my dog obsessive. Only dog owners who experience this bond get it. Dogs are social animals like people are social. It is a known fact all social creatures possess emotions which enable a social group to bond in their support of one another. The strength of love in a social group is the glue which holds them together. But with dogs, unlike humans, this bond can never be broken. One has only to scratch behind your dog's ears or rub their belly to feel this bond in the making. The emotional life of a dog far exceeds the human tendency for bonds made and broken. While people come and go from our lives, our dog remains steadfast. We love our dogs so much because they seem to understand us in ways few people ever can. This understanding is deeply emotional, while simultaneously elevated to spiritual. How is it, why is it, our dogs love us so completely beyond most people? They are doing their Divine job for which they were designed and chosen, and to which we respond in doing our job to love them. And in turn, they

they respond to us in kind. It is a good trade.

"If you don't own a dog, at least one, there is not necessarily anything wrong with you, but there may be something wrong with your life."

— Roger Caras

As we humans awaken to the Divine as spiritual beings, we come face to face with the shadow of ambivalence in ourselves and others. We are caught in a seemingly endless cycle of doubting our own and others' capacity for love, while our dog is clear about its friends and enemies. Freud explained it this way, *"...dogs love their friends and bite their enemies, quite unlike people, who are incapable of pure love and always have to mix love and hate in their object relations."* While our dog's love and loyalty is undeniable, we cannot forget their wild ancestry. Some sweet dogs can turn mean. Though this can be the result of a medical issue, dogs are still wild predators with territorial dominance and possessive tendencies and thus, aggression can surface in even the sweetest dog.

Dogs can be fiercely protective and aggressive as they distinguish between friends and enemies. When we encounter a mean dog, we can quickly forget their loyal and loving nature. We are vulnerable to the wolf in dogs when they distinguish us as the enemy. Dogs get a bad rap when the wolf in them shows up. Many people are extremely afraid of dogs as a result. Some dog breeds seem to have had the wolf bred out of them more than others, while other dogs are bred and trained to be mean, such as guard dogs. There are certain breeds we know to be wary of, while others can be embraced affectionately. Unfortunately as well, some dog owners can be cruel and abusive to their dogs. This causes confusion and distrust for a dog as to friend and foe. Dogs are willing to do whatever job we give them—whether it is to guard, protect, lead the blind, or simply be a cherished friend. Dogs that love and are loved in return are very clear as to who is a friend or an enemy. In spite of their wildness, dogs above all other animals in the wild chose to be our companions. They willingly tame their wild nature to bestow upon us an understanding and devotion from which we mutually benefit. While ironically we may believe we have domesticated dogs, it is the gifts they bring to us which allow us to reclaim our natural selves as loving and gentle beings.

"No matter how close we are to another person, few human relationships are as free from strife, disagreement, and frustration as is the relationship you have with a good dog. Few human beings give of themselves to another as a dog gives of itself. I also suspect that we cherish dogs because their unblemished souls make us wish—consciously or unconsciously—that we were as innocent as they are, and make us yearn for a place where innocence is universal and where the meanness, the betrayals, and the cruelties of this world are unknown."

— Dean Koontz

We may not realize a dog's purpose is far more than retrieving the Frisbee, herding cattle or guarding the fort. All dogs have a history of having been bred for a specific purpose: hunting and bird dogs flush, track and retrieve the hunted—cattle dogs herd sheep and cattle—guard dogs protect, and so forth. As humans, we are not so different in that we are born with the instincts to guide, heal, protect and serve. We associate living our purpose with a sense of peace and fulfillment, while not living our purpose can bring confusion and despair. Yet, our dogs can forego the purpose for which they were bred, and simply show up in our lives to bring us love and joy. In doing so, they teach us the valuable lesson that our own life purpose is ultimately defined by the love and joy we carry in our hearts. Forsaking our life's purpose does not diminish this joy and love.

The experience of unconditional love with our dogs will inevitably lead us to the God in our dog, and to the God in ourselves. What a gift. Our journey with our dog is the journey into our own heart. It is sweetened by their sheer delight of being in our presence as their easy, joyful spirit flows into every adventure. They gratefully accept us and trust in us as loving masters.

Stories with a
Down Under Dog

Life with Tapa

Tapa came to me in the shadows of the Blue Ridge Mountains of Virginia on an evening in September 2005. She was 13 weeks old. My oldest son was heading over the mountain to look at Blue

Heeler pups, and asked me to join him. I was reluctant. Since losing my last dog in 2001, a yellow Lab that lived with me in Santa Fe, New Mexico, I had been dogless. I knew if I went with him, I would melt in the face of sweet temptation to scoop up a new little puppy. I went. I scooped up Tapa.

She was born on a working cattle farm. Her mama was a true working cattle dog whom I met. My son chose her brother, Chile, to live and work on our family cattle farm. We brought them both home where they hid beneath a living room chair. It was late, we had no dog food so I made scrambled eggs which I pushed beneath the chair, and dinner was devoured. Home was beneath this chair for the night, and most of the next day. It took long, stretched out arms to give belly rubs to finally lure them out. Once they ventured out, they never went back. Double trouble had begun. It would be some time before I would realize how appropriately I had named Tapa, which means *"little bite"* in Spanish. She would consistently live up to her name.

Tapa traveled with me from Virginia in 2006 back to New Mexico, down to Mexico twice in the winter of 2008-2009 and then to Florida in 2012. She was the best traveling dog ever. Road checks were common in Mexico. Whenever I got stopped, and was requested to step out of the truck, I would reply, "Mi perro es muy bravo." My dog is very mean. When I said the word "bravo" with emphasis, it always signaled Tapa to show her teeth, which she did. I never did have to step out of my truck—not once.

I was always amazed how fast Tapa learned. When I wanted to teach her something new, she would perk up her ears and give me a long, deep gaze with her full attention. She was so eager to understand and learn. Sometimes she would get playful, distracted and pretend she was not learning. Later on, out of the blue, she would prove she had been listening.

Tapa was fiercely protective of me and her territory. Despite how much I worked with her, I could never ease her barking when strangers came to the house. In some ways, I did not want to discourage this completely as she was a good guard dog. I never had to worry about anyone breaking into the house as her presence would certainly make a burglar think twice. Eventually, she came to distinguish my friends from strangers. When I knew a friend was coming to visit, I would tell her by name who was coming. She completely understood a friend was coming soon, and would endearingly head for the door to sit and wait. She rarely barked when they arrived. Tapa always knew the people I welcomed into my life, and she in turn cared about them. Her defensive guard diminished in their presence to be replaced by offerings of affection. During gatherings with my women friends, Tapa was so delighted to participate as one of the girls. Her sweet, vocal howls were always a sign she was happy to be in your company. She especially loved parties, along with all the music and often sang along.

Tapa knew her boundaries when it came to  aggression, but there were just some dogs, and people, she simply would not tolerate in her space. She had a greater trust of women than men. While she instinctively wanted to herd every person into the house upon arrival, she rarely nipped at a woman's heels, and almost always nipped at certain men. I could see immediately the people she trusted, and those she did not. Though I never witnessed her bite another person, or dog, she would take those little bites at the heels or the hands of men walking about or working in her protective space. She was serious about her territory, and I had to become somewhat stern about keeping an eye on her. Once outside her territory in neutral zone, Tapa went off duty and relaxed. I did, however, always have to monitor her closely around small children since she had not grown up with them.

For all of her intensity in her protective role, Tapa was equally intense in her sweet showering of affection, her desire to be closely connected and her willingness for play and adventure. She followed me everywhere, and would often wake from what appeared to be a deep sleep and move to wherever I was hanging out. Like many dogs, she always sensed when I would be getting ready to go out, following my every move in anticipation of the welcomed words, "*Let's go.*" or the dreaded words, "*You stay.*"

Always upon my return, she would be waiting to greet me at the door with the ecstasy of a long, lost love which melted my heart—a pair of my socks or jeans on her dog bed were the endearing sign of how she had missed me. I marveled endlessly at her range of expressions, from her sphinx pose with crossed front legs and closed eyes, to her spread eagle on her back, to her sudden lightening runs which spoke of a wild, runaway wind. This was a girl of true grit, depth and character whose every breath was a celebration of being alive, and loving to be by my side.

A Bit about Blue Heelers

If you are not familiar with these amazing, warm, smart, strong and sweet dogs from down under called Blue Heelers, here is a bit of history about these Dingo descendants. Then I will tell stories.

Australian cattle dogs, also known as heelers, are a unique dog breed. Unlike many domesticated dogs, they have not been subjected to abundant inbreeding or overbreeding. Heelers remain a very pure breed. Their Australian roots are connected to the wild Dingo dog, and their herding instincts are very strong. They were bred to endure the job of herding cattle across large expanses of land in extreme hot and cold weather conditions. They accomplish their herding tasks by biting the heels of the cattle. This is a genetic instinct that cannot be changed. If you own a Heeler as a pet instead of a working dog, you will need to find ways to limit and distract your Heeler from natu-

rally wanting to herd people. Tapa herded me into the shower and hot tub regularly. It is critical that Heelers are well socialized in their first year to prevent them from becoming overly aggressive.

Heelers are extremely tough dogs. They will hike with you in hot climates without needing or wanting drinks of water, and hike with you in extreme cold without a single shiver. Their coats are designed to insulate them from the cold, yet keep them cool in the heat. They do not like humid conditions, but favor high and dry climates like their native country of Australia. Most Heelers love the snow, but not all Heelers love being in the water. Tapa loved the water, but her brother in Virginia won't have anything to do with water. Heelers are energetic, always ready for adventure and to play. As a pet, they require a lot of exercise and play time. They will become quite put out with you if you coop them up all day, and ignore their need to romp and play. Do not be fooled by their tolerance for this, fueled by their deep loyalty and love for you, as you will not be doing their health and happiness justice. Your Heeler needs to express and share his/her high energy love for life. If given such freedoms, you will see this dog shine with keen intelligence, as well as athletic superiority and agility.

Heelers come in two colors, red and blue. I have yet to see evidence of a major distinction in character traits between the two colors. Cattle dogs are happiest in an open, natural environment where they can run, explore and feel like they have a job to do. They are eager to play ball, Frisbee, swim and welcome any athletic, agility or endurance training challenges. These dogs are so smart, and you can train them to do almost anything within a matter of days. Their loyalty is such many folks call them "Velcro" dogs. They want to be by your side constantly.

Tapa taught me many wonders; from her mischievous puppy days collecting piles of shoes, scarves, undies, jeans and whatever else she found to be her favorite things—all scattered into piles throughout the house—moving from one to another while chewing; to her glory days chasing Frisbees into the ocean and riding the waves, and even in her weak, sick, sad days wasting away with acute kidney disease. Following are stories and lessons about the most devoted companion I ever had.

The Big Snow

In the fall of 2006, Tapa traveled with me back to New Mexico from Virginia. I lived in an awesome glass home perched on the mountain side like an eagle's nest with hundred mile views. In December, just a few days before Christmas, it snowed...and snowed...and snowed. When it finally stopped, there was more than four feet blanketing the ground. This was Tapa's first snow. She loved it, disappearing into the trees and returning with frozen nostrils, ears and smiling. On the morning after the snow was finally done falling, I opened the door to let her out to do her business. She returned quickly, and when she came inside, she spun around in circles, looked at me and howled. She had never done this before, and I just smiled and giggled at her new antics I assumed were inspired by the snow. She sat by the door, howled and spun around some more. She then turned to paw the door,

seemingly wanting to go back outside again, so I let her out. She ran to the edge of the deck, spun around and howled again. She looked towards the trees, then back at me, howled some more then ran towards me, then back towards the trees where she sat and gave me one of those looks. In that moment, upon seeing her sitting against a four foot high backdrop of snow, I realized she could not navigate through this wall of snow to do her business. I went to find a shovel, whereupon she spun around in joy knowing I had finally understood what she needed...a nice, long path dug for her into the trees.

From this day forward, whenever Tapa had something important to say, she would spin around and howl. She had taught me how to listen.

Walking the Ranch

I was the co-owner of a beautiful 125 acre ranch in the pristine Galisteo basin south of Santa Fe from 2006 to 2010. It was a dream come true for me. I had plans to build a solar home, and be a steward of this special land. It never happened. But for four

years, I enjoyed long walks here with Tapa where we were both in a slice of heaven.

Tapa came to know the road to the ranch. The minute the truck wheels hit the gravel road, she started pacing in the back seat until I put the window down for her to channel this excitement with her face in the wind. The second we arrived and she jumped out of the truck, she was gone. I would catch up with her along the path to the creek. The Galisteo creek ran through the ranch. This was very special in the high, dry desert where water was scarce. There was also a lake on the land which would fill in heavy rains. Most of the time it remained empty due to ongoing drought conditions, but once in September it filled for my birthday party I had planned at the ranch beneath the cottonwood trees. Everyone swam, canoed and kayaked in the lake. It was quite incredible. The creek managed to have a steady bit of water in it year round, and only ran high if abundant spring or summer rains came. It was perfect for Tapa to play in. The creek was at the bottom of a steep embankment where it meandered like a snake for 40-50 miles. Tapa and I would walk the twists and

turns for hours, resting beneath Russian olive trees that provided welcome shade along the creek's edge. There were a few special spots where the creek's sandy bottom was exposed in great expanses that reminded me of the beach by the ocean. We would park on the shady beach by a pool of water where I began the game of throwing rocks up and down the creek. Tapa would chase them as a reason to run and run, splashing through the water where she often dunked her head while running, or just completely submerged to cool off. She was often covered in mud, and could not have been happier.

There were lots of snakes on the ranch, including rattlesnakes. I carried a long stick just in case of an unwanted encounter. One late afternoon in summer, we were heading for the creek. Tapa was usually up ahead exploring and scouting, but never failed to look back often to check on me. Suddenly, she ran back towards me, and began her spinning and howling routine. I knew she was talking to me, and had something important to say. We kept walking slowly, and she seemed very anxious. About a hundred yards further, she started barking which was followed by the distinct sound of a rattler. I spotted the snake about three feet away nestled in the grass just off the path. It was a big one. I took off running so Tapa would follow me to prevent an encounter on her part with this big snake. Further down the path, I stopped to pet her and thank her for being such a smart, protective, watchful dog. I told her "good girl" over and over until she pranced onward with her head held high, so pleased to have a job she did well. I was so grateful to have her alertness and warnings for the presence of snakes. I relaxed more whenever we detoured off the path to walk the large, grassy fields where snakes could easily hide. I put my full faith in Tapa that she would stay alert and warn me without getting bit. This was our first rattlesnake encounter, and it would not be the last.

Rattlesnake Close Encounter

I only worried about rattlesnake encounters when we were walking the ranch or hiking in the hills behind the house. I certainly never worried about them when I was at home. But one morning, that all changed. I was getting ready to head into town for an appointment. I was looking for my reading glasses, then recalled I left them on the front porch. I opened the big glass front door, spotted my glasses behind the door on the bench, picked them up and when I turned around, there was a large five foot rattlesnake half way into my house through the open door. Mind you I had just walked out the same door five seconds ago. I was so stunned, I froze. But my mind rapidly assessed the situation with the snake on its way into my house, with Tapa lying on the floor maybe 20 feet away and the idea of this snake all the way inside was not going to be a good scene. I could not let this snake all the way inside, so I gently pushed the door closed on him, knowing it would either send it all the way in or startle it and make it retreat.

As the door closed on it, the whole front of its body reared straight up in the air, turned on a dime and was staring me down. As I slowly started moving backwards, it reared up further and struck out at me whereupon I leaped backwards, fell over a big rock I used as a doorstop and came down hard on the concrete patio. I didn't stop there, but scrambled off the patio onto the gravel. My heart was pounding as I watched the snake coil up in front of the still open front door with Tapa right inside barking like mad. The back door was locked, the only window I could squeeze through was four feet from the front door and all I could think about was how to get the front door closed before Tapa and this snake had an encounter.

I had no choice but to get a long stick, go back to the porch and attempt to shut the door without getting a snake bite. Then once Tapa was safe, I could try to fit through the open window and pray the snake did not come after me. I broke a long branch off a nearby tree, and slowly made my way towards the front door. As I raised the stick, the rattler raised its tail high above its coiled body and began rattling. Tapa went nuts. She quickly stood guard right at the door barking aggressively so as to let the snake know it was not a good idea to come inside. Perhaps now the snake was con-fused as to which one of us to go after, with one protector behind and one in front. I took a deep breath, heaved the stick at the front door, saw it close, backed up fast and ran. The rattler had stayed put rattling. I got another stick and slowly moved towards the window. Facing the snake with stick in hand, I removed the screen and squeezed my way in through the narrow opening. Once inside, I shut the window, locked the front door and collapsed on the floor.

As I laid there, I could now feel the pain from my fall on the patio. I got up, made an ice pack and then walked to the front door where the rattler was contently coiled. I did not know what to make of this visitation. I sat down on the floor in front of the door, just inches away from it through the glass. Tapa came to sit next to me, looked at the snake, showed her teeth, growled and then went crazy barking when the snake resumed its rattling. She kept coming over to me, nudging me, as if to tell me to please move away from the door. But I was intrigued with this rare opportunity to observe a rattlesnake at such a close proximity and safe behind the glass door. So I sat there staring at this rattler while it stared back. I was asking questions in the process. Why was this rattlesnake coming into my house? Where the hell was it when I walked out the front door? How the hell did I miss seeing it? Its energy was so intense and powerful. As I sat there in communion with the snake, I felt as though it was imparting me with some of its essence, its energy and power. It began to freak me out. My hip was really hurting by now and I was emotionally drained. I called to make an appointment with my chiropractor. They said that they could see me in an hour, so I headed into town leaving all the windows and doors of the house locked tight.

Incredibly, upon our return, there was that rattlesnake all stretched out on the front porch snoozing in the shade. Tapa and I came in through the back door. I went to do a Google search for snake medicine. It stayed there all day, occasionally moving as the sun and shade moved. Around 7:30 pm, I saw it slowly slither off the front porch and out into the front field. For weeks I was on edge, looking everywhere before I opened the front door or working in the garden. All the while, I was pondering on the snake medicine messages and meanings of transformation: death and rebirth, renewal, transitions, power, strength and the healing of the feminine. At the time, I could not see the magnitude of the transition my life was taking, though I knew change was clearly in the cards. I made my peace with the understanding perhaps this rattlesnake had come to prepare me, strengthen me in some way for the change to come. But Tapa and I were not done with rattlesnakes yet.

Rattlesnake Life or Death

In late August, several months after the rattlesnake close encounter, I decided to take a new hike with Tapa. A friend had told me about some beautiful rock canyons down past the railroad tracks. It would be a good four to five hour hike there and back. I filled my day pack with all the essentials, and we left the house close to 1 pm. At the bottom of my long driveway, I stopped to talk with a neighbor who asked where I was headed. When I told him, he warned me there were a lot of rattlesnakes in those rock canyons and to be careful. Great! About a hundred yards later, I turned around and went back to the house for my pistol, a Smith and Wesson .38 revolver. After what I had already experienced, I was not up for another close encounter. With my pistol now in my pack, we set off. I loved new adventures, and Tapa loved them even more.

We hiked quite a long ways along the railroad tracks, then veered away across a large field and headed up into the hills. About an hour and a half later, we entered the rock canyons. I could see way up near the top of the ridge an outcropping of small trees, and made that our destination. We were hiking up and over and down these huge red rock boulders. Tapa was far more agile and faster than me at navigating our way through the rocks. She was up ahead and out of sight when I heard her barking...and barking. She suddenly appeared atop a huge rock, and I was not happy to see her do the spin and howl act. She took off, I followed and two to three big rocks later, I came upon Tapa barking within a few feet of a big rattlesnake partially coiled on a big rock with his head up and tail rattling.

Here we go again, I thought. I was scared to death it was going to strike Tapa, and I did not waste one second in pulling out my pistol. I called and called her to come, but she would not budge so I shot a round in the air hoping to get her attention. No luck. I moved in closer, aimed for the top of the rattler's back, fired and missed. It looked pissed. I took no more chances, moved within six feet behind it and just to the side of Tapa. I shot high and missed, then aimed low and hit it in the head. Tapa took off. I was stunned. What was the deal with these rattlesnake encounters? If the message was about change and transformation, I was certain now it was going to be really big. The snake was dead. I picked it up near its tail, laid it in the shade of a rock and went to find Tapa. The grove of trees was not too far, and I found her here in the shade. I did not know what to say to her since she persisted in an encounter that could have killed her. I thought about the last rattler encounter—how she clearly got the message that these creatures could be dangerous so she was just doing her job. I doused her head with water, we both drank and rested before the long hike home.

As we passed the crime scene descending the ridge, I decided a crazy thing. I carried an old gutting knife with me so I cut the last foot or so off the snake, then buried the rest of it. I said a prayer asking for the rattlesnakes to please let this be enough, blessed them and moved on. When we got home, I laid the snake part onto the outdoor table, and stared at it against the setting sun while sipping a glass of wine. I was feeling mixed emotions; remorse for having killed this snake and gratitude I had brought my pistol. If this rattler had bitten Tapa, I do not know what I would have done. I let the remorse go. I recalled having eaten snake once as a girl at camp, and I did not remember it tasting bad. Many shamans talked about animal encounters—about eating a piece of them to embody their energy and message. I was feeling desperate. So I cut a small piece and sautéed it in butter and garlic. Maybe now these rattlesnake encounters would cease. I was done.

The next morning I laid the rattle on the outdoor table in the sun. These snake rattles have an eerie feel to them with smooth, strong, triangular shapes stacked on one another. Every time a snake sheds its skin, it gets another new triangular shape called a button. When the snake rattles, the buttons separate just enough so they knock against one another to make the rattle sound. When I held the rattle for the first time, it felt like it was from some way out, alien planet. I wanted to keep it, like a totem hunters collect from their kills. But later in the day, Tapa had snatched the rattle off the table, and chewed into tiny pieces. And so it was…the end of our rattlesnake adventures. Coyotes would be next.

Coyote Encounter

New Mexico is home to many coyotes. It is common to hear coyote serenades at night, particularly on the full moon, and to see packs of them moving across a distant hill side. Sometimes you would see one crossing the street in the middle of town. Tapa and I often heard or saw them on our many hikes. In 2004, I had my own shocking coyote encounter which left me intrigued, but not afraid of coyotes. Though there were no stories of coyotes ever killing a person, there were plenty involving the deaths of cats and dogs who succumbed to coyote encounters.

It was late October. Tapa and I were enjoying a warm, Indian summer evening on the front porch. The sun had dipped behind the ridge, and the cool shadows of darkness were moving in for the night. I heard my teapot whistle, and went inside to make tea. Within moments, I heard Tapa bark and take off across the front field. She was on a mission…and I hoped it was not coyotes. I had often seen a pack of five come down the ridge across the driveway, and cross the road at the edge of the front field. I went to the porch and called her. Then I heard the barks, howls and growls of a dog fight, and knew she was in trouble. I did not waste any time. I loaded my pistol, grabbed a flash light and took off running across the front field. As I approached the fight, I saw Tapa engaged with three coyotes. She was fighting two in front of her while the third one was trying to pin her down from behind. I shot two quick rounds in the air, and all three coyotes quickly scattered and fled. Tapa did not go after them as I could see she was quite shaken. She ran back to the house.

When I got her inside, I could see the damage done, and was immediately grateful it was minimal. One of her ears was torn and bleeding, and she had a good scratch across her nose. But the coyote who pinned her from behind had left its mark on her backside. She had long rows of skin showing on both sides, and a small puncture by her left hip. I was a wreck, and she was pacing the living room while stopping to growl by the front door. I let us both calm down before I began doctoring her wounds. I gave Tapa a gentle, but firm talking to that night, and hoped she had learned her lesson not to tango with these guys and let them be. The next morning I could see she was sore from her battle, and took her to the vet to be checked over. It was days before her soreness passed, and months before her hair grew back in to hide the coyote claw marks. The vet was amazed at Tapa's toughness to take on the coyotes, and while most dogs will bark aggressively at them, few would actually take them on. She assured me my intervention had saved her life. She explained how coyotes pin their prey from behind, often leading them on a chase while other coyotes suddenly attacked from behind. The vet said she would be surprised if Tapa would engage with the coyotes again. Tapa would prove her wrong.

Coyote Chase

I awoke one winter morning early to a soft snow falling. I let Tapa outside while I made coffee. With coffee in hand, I walked to the front door and stood watching the snow gently fall as the golden light of the morning sun pierced through a cloud to illuminate everything into a sparkling winter wonderland. It was just magical.

Then I suddenly spotted the pack of coyotes, five of them, heading down the ridge to cross the road. Tapa was very near the road. I opened the front door and called her. She turned and came running. About thirty yards from the house she stopped and got wind of them. Damn! She looked back, spotted them and took off. I dropped my coffee cup, ran inside, grabbed my pistol, put on my Ugg boots and took off running. Tapa was already out of sight. I followed the tracks in the snow up one hill, down and up another. I am thinking all along what the vet said; how the coyotes set up the chase, split up, and attack from behind.

As I came to the top of the third hill, Tapa appeared. She was looking very pleased with herself. We stood at the top of the hill, and spotted the pack of coyotes moving quickly up a distant hill. I looked at Tapa, she looked at me. I shook my head, but I could see she was driven to do her job. She liked her protection work. She was not afraid of the coyotes. She was afraid of not doing her job of instinctively protecting her territory like her wild ancestors. The wild coyotes were perhaps a strong reminder of this. On our walk back to the house, I thought it might be time to move closer into town for my sanity and Tapa's security. I was getting my fill of these wild animal adventures.

Within minutes of walking into the house, one of my neighbors called. He asked if everything was OK as he had seen me running across the snow-covered hill by his house in my bathrobe with a gun in my hand. Months later, we moved closer to town. I could not control Tapa's deep commitment to her job as coyote chaser. She was clearly not willing to quit her job.

Safe Haven

In our new safe haven, we had a nice break from rattlesnakes and coyotes. Our walks took us through long arroyos, and along well trodden trails through fields where horses grazed.

I found myself reflecting on all these encounters, the meaning and message of rattlesnake and coyote medicine. I was living in the enchanted land of Native American myths and legends about many of the animals here. Clearly, the Native Americans had these animal legends based on their actual experiences with them, and most likely these myths formed the basis of some good storytelling. I had an opportunity one day to go with a friend to meet a great granddaughter of Geronimo. She was an extraordinary woman. I noticed next to her chair a walking stick with a rattlesnake carved into it—the head of the snake being at the top where one would grip the stick. I inquired. She told me rattlesnakes had powerful, psychic medicine. She said they brought messages to pay attention to one's gut feelings since they traveled this earth on their bellies where they could feel and sense everything around them.

She confirmed that they often foretold of big transformations, but also that rattlesnakes were known as the protector of women. Now I felt guilty for killing one, and told her my stories. In response to the first one, she said this rattlesnake came to my home to warn me of my need for protection, most likely from something of which I was unaware or had yet to occur. She felt the rattler could have easily struck me if he had wanted to, but he did not. It was bringing me the power of its presence to alert me and get my attention, and that it stayed all day to be sure I got the message. It definitely got my attention, but I was still unsure of what I needed protection from. To the second story, she said whatever I was needing protection from was going to ultimately feel like a death to me. The rattler had sacrificed itself so that I would live through this death, this big transformation; by eating part of it, I had assured some integration of its power and continuous protection. Tapa's confrontation with the rattler and dissection of the rattle indicated she would play a big part in this transformation.

I later followed up on more coyote medicine. Coyote is known as the trickster, the paradox of wisdom and folly, the messenger of an honest need to look at our own actions. Who was out to trick me? Was I going to choose the wise path or become the fool? What did I honestly need to see about what I was doing? I did not understand it all then, but I do now.

The house I had been living in became so symbolic for these rattlesnake and coyote encounters. Circumstances in my personal life did indeed reveal close people in my life exploiting the trickster energy of coyote to which I was not paying close attention. I was putting my trust in the wrong people, which in the end made me feel like a fool. I was not choosing wisely. In retrospect, my actions were full of resistance to the truth which resulted in my betrayal. Here was coyote showing up as the trickster, the paradox of the wisdom I thought I had only to become the fool. Here was rattlesnake showing up as the protector, trying to alert me to the betrayals I would endure, and the subsequent transformation of my life as a result. I would soon embrace the huge change of leaving my home of sixteen years in the high desert, and move to the tropics. It was the death of the life I had known and loved.

The Final Journey

The move to Miami was a very tough adjustment for us both, but especially Tapa. Fortunately, we both loved the ocean. I had taken her on several occasions to the ocean in Mexico. It was here she first met the sea and surprised me with her love of the water. Like in Mexico, we would go to the beach where I would throw the ball or Frisbee in the ocean for her to retrieve until one of us had enough, then she would sit beneath my beach umbrella while I went swimming. She did not budge from this spot, regardless of people and other dogs going by. Her eyes stayed fixed on me in the ocean the entire time. I was so impressed with her obedience to stay put so I could swim.

The ocean brought healing to us both. Rattlesnakes and coyotes were replaced with raccoons, tropical singing birds and squawking parrots. But I could tell Tapa was missing her long four to five hour hikes in the mountains and arroyos. So was I...and thought to myself when the time was right, perhaps we would return to the high desert. It never crossed my mind there was a danger lurking here which would prove more deadly than rattlesnakes and coyotes. It was a complete shock when she contracted Leptospirosis.

From almost dying from the Lepto, to making a comeback and finally losing her battle with kidney disease, Tapa was a true warrior of life. She taught me how to be strong, to not back down and to embrace life, to welcome every new experience and adventure, to be kind, patient, stay present and to love deeply. Her faith and trust in me was an endless soothing balm to my soul. I was deeply shaken at my core when she contracted her illness. I did not know if I could save her this time. I felt myself dig deep for the strength of that rattlesnake medicine. Here was a big transforma-

tion in which Tapa was playing a major role. I struggled to become my own warrior. I thought my own emotional death was enough. Why now did Tapa have to face her own?

I cared for her as best as I could. I know she knew that. When I realized our time together was coming to an end, I felt my heart crack...and into that crack poured all the love and light Tapa had left in her. I soaked it up, and showered it back onto her right up until her last breath.

She fought this disease with the same courage she battled coyotes and rattlesnakes. She would have fought it to the bitter end if I had let her, but I could not watch her continually suffer. She knew she was losing this fight. Yet, she would poise herself with grace despite her sad eyes, and accept it was her time to go. Her job was done.

I sit in silence often in her favorite orange chair, and reflect on all our adventures together. I realize she carried me through some of the hardest years of my life with the presence of her joy and strength, and what a better woman I am now from having known and shared her love and courage. We journey separately now, but I feel her every day and every night. She comes to me when I close my eyes. Her spirit is alive and well. She tells me there is a gift for me in her transformation from life to death...the gift of my own transformation now from death to life. In the dark night of my soul, I had lost the man I loved, the ranch I loved, the dreams I loved and finally, the dog I loved. Tapa is my guide now to welcome a new life and trust again, to forgive myself, to gratefully accept my life and all it has brought to me and to keep loving with all my heart.

For my sweet Tapa, I will carry on.

Tapa's Illness

I made the decision to move to Florida in 2012. My youngest son and his wife live in Miami, so this is where I landed. I knew it was going to be hard on Tapa. She was an outback dog use to rolling in the snow, swimming in rivers and lakes and hiking for miles into the wilderness and in sandy arroyos. The high, dry desert climate suited her. She was not happy here in the hot, humid summers. We dealt with it by taking early 7 a.m. walks and swims at the beach, or early evening walks to the bay. In March, I decided to explore a national park here in Miami with lots of trails. My son and I took Tapa there the first time the end of February and she just ran and ran. I returned again the next weekend with a friend where we hiked the longest trail in the park. Tapa was a happy camper.

About ten days after this hike, Tapa began vomiting yellow bile. She had never done this before. I took her to the vet who said she looked very healthy, probably got into something and sent me home with some meds. I declined doing blood work or more tests at the time. I was not overly worried. She had only been sick once before and healed quickly. A few days after starting the meds, she stopped vomiting. I thought we were on the mend until the third day after finishing the meds when she was back vomiting yellow bile. It was back to the vet.

The vet said it was time to check blood along with a sonogram to rule out any intestinal obstructions. She was clear of any blockages, and I waited for her blood work results. The next afternoon the vet called to tell me Tapa's blood indicated she was in multiple organ failure, she was very sick and to bring her right in. I was stunned. I was told she would be staying at least five nights in the animal hospital while they started her on IV fluids, did more tests and worked to save her life.

It all happened so fast. Soon after, the vet called to say Tapa either had cancer, poisoning or an infectious disease as these were the only causes of multiple organ failure. They were doing tests to find out which one was the culprit. He told me to check my yard and house, and to consider where I had been in the last two weeks for any possible exposure to poisons. I did my due diligence researching all the plants, trees and flowers to discover the very poisonous Sago Palm in my backyard, three of them. I saved a clipping and dug them up. I thought of everywhere else I had been, and what she might have been exposed to. I could think of nothing.

Cancer was ruled out, followed by poisoning. However, the infectious disease blood tests came back revealing Leptospirosis. This was not good news. Leptospirosis comes from a bacteria found in the urine of raccoons, opossums, skunks, squirrels and other wildlife. Dogs are exposed simply by sniffing the urine, or by swimming in contaminated still water. Infection sets in between 8-10 days after exposure. It did not take me long to realize Tapa had most likely been exposed on our last hike to Oleta National Park on March 7th. She had started vomiting exactly nine days later. I will go into greater detail about Leptospirosis in the next chapter, but suffice it to say here, only about 40 percent of all dogs survive this infection. The survival rate depends upon how quickly the disease is diagnosed and treated before irreversible damage is done. We had already lost another 10 days while treating her for vomiting without realizing she was infected. Though the vet had started her on penicillin IV fluids, it was three weeks before she was diagnosed. Tapa came home on April 4th, and we began the treatment to kill this damn Lepto.

The Long Hard Road

The treatment for Lepto is an antibiotic called doxycycline, a very potent drug that completely flattened poor Tapa. It was a three week treatment during which time she parked on the blanket covered couch, and just slept. She was also given a med to calm her stomach from the side effects of the doxy, and I had to syringe this into her mouth. Her breathing was hard and fast, and she would barely eat. On the evening of the third night home, I woke suddenly after midnight to find Tapa cold, listless and barely breathing. She did not respond when I touched her, and I felt she was leaving. I wrapped myself around her under a blanket, and began rocking and chanting. I have no idea of the words I was chanting, what they meant or from where they came. I prayed she would stay with me, and held her all night while these mystical sounds poured forth from the depths of my being. I awoke in the morning to her licking my face.

Something shifted that night. I believe Tapa made the decision to fight for her life and to trust me in the process. She became more responsive, found a bit more energy and began to eat more. But each time I gave her the doxy, it knocked her out and she would sleep for hours. Around the 10th day of treatment, we took an afternoon nap on a rainy day. When we got up, Tapa was shaking and ran into the wall, then another wall and could not find the door. She could not see. I led her down the hall and outside where she wandered lost around the yard. I brought her in, parked her on the couch next to me and began a Google search for Lepto and the doxy associated with blindness. I read the Lepto could cause blindness but that it was most common in horses that were infected. The symptoms of blindness were a result of the bacteria attacking the soft tissues and creating inflammation. I was relieved to read that, in dogs, the blindness was usually temporary. I called the vet who said she had never heard of this, and to give it a few days. So we waited. Poor Tapa was desperately upset from not being able to see. I applied cold compresses over her eyes to reduce the inflammation which seemed to calm her. I kept talking to her and assuring her that this would pass. Little by little each day, her eyesight returned.

Zoonotic Disease

One of the most unsettling aspects of Leptospirosis is its zoonotic nature—meaning it is contagious to both other dogs and humans. This fact increased my work load tenfold and imposed limitations. I had to be conscious of sterilizing everything, constantly, right down to spraying the grass with Clorox where she urinated. The Lepto was shedding out of her body through her urine, and any remaining live bacteria could potentially stay contagiously active for several days, especially in wet grass or water. I could not have any friends over with their dogs, nor could I take Tapa with me to anyone's home. We endured over three weeks of isolation.

More Complications

As we were approaching the end of the second week of treatment, Tapa began periods of shaking, coughing and periodic vomiting. Again, it was back to the vet. We came home with cough and vomiting meds along with IV fluids and needles. I had to learn how to administer fluids regularly. It was dreadful. My son put in the effort to come by three times a week to help me. Eventually, I learned how to do this myself. I ordered thinner needles so Tapa would not jump nor yelp every time I had to give her fluids.

Tapa was really struggling to handle the doxycycline. I hated the idea of giving her even more meds on top of the doxy. I had raised my boys on homeopathy instead of allopathic medicine, and began to consider the idea of a homeopathic vet. I found one in the area, and made an appointment. He was very helpful, and agreed she was not tolerating the doxy at all. We only had a short time left on it so we began splitting the doses to give her some relief. It helped her tremendously, and she began to eat more. He gave me some remedies to help her with nausea and vomiting. I was hopeful we could continue to treat her without so many drug meds.

The homeopathic vet wanted me to redo the Lepto test. There are six strains of Lepto, of which Tapa had three, but her numbers were low. If in fact she had been recently exposed to Lepto, then a second test would reveal elevated spikes in these numbers. He wanted to rule out the possibility that some other underlying issue could be going on so he would know best how to help her. We had to wait another week for the results.

At the conclusion of the three week doxy treatments, we returned to the regular vet to recheck Tapa's blood and more. She was diagnosed as very anemic with high blood pressure. She also had fluid in her abdomen and her kidney counts were still not good. The good news was that her liver and pancreas had stabilized and returned to normal function. More meds were given to maintain normal blood pressure, drain her abdomen and heal her anemia. The vet then explained what we were facing; Tapa's kidneys were damaged. How much they were compromised yet, he did not know. It was now a waiting game to see if her kidneys would respond. Every month that passed without an improvement would indicate kidney damage beyond repair. It was imperative for her survival that her kidneys begin to stabilize. She would have to be on these meds for life along with the fluids if her kidneys did not respond sufficiently. If we could get her kidney count within a certain range, we could manage the kidney damage with meds and diet for her to live longer. Kidneys are not a rejuvenating organ like the liver so kidney damage is permanent. Our hope was that Tapa's kidneys would recover to the point we could manage her kidney disease successfully.

Improvement

Tapa improved drastically on these meds. Her energy and spark returned, she began eating and playing like normal and we resumed our beach walks. I was still giving her fluids three to four times a week to assist her kidneys in doing their job. Her improvement spurred my enthusiasm to do everything I possibly could to make her stronger. I researched canine kidney disease for hours at a time to find every gem to help us with this battle. I found recipes and herbs to help her. I began making all of her food: organic chicken, turkey with rice or yams topped with broth, coconut or salmon oil, detox herbs, ground flaxseed, chia seeds and doggie greens. She loved it and devoured it. I even made her homemade dog biscuits. By May 10th, all her vomiting had stopped, and she was chasing the ball on the beach and riding the waves like her old self. I was elated to see her happy again. I did not return to the homeopathic vet as I felt we were making good progress in spite of the vet meds.

The second Lepto test came back with no elevated spikes in her numbers, indicating a recent exposure to Lepto was now questionable. She may have been exposed to it many months prior, her body had been trying to fight it off and finally succumbed which caused the acute attack. I had no blood profile at all for Tapa in the past so there was no way for us to know if an underlying issue had been present, and we had nothing to compare. Despite the doubt now of a recent Lepto exposure, we were faced with kidney disease. It became somewhat irrelevant at this point as to the cause. The focus was to try and strengthen her kidneys to prevent kidney failure.

The beginning of June we returned to the vet for more blood work. The vet was pleased to see Tapa doing so well. It was what we had been hoping for and we were optimistic her blood tests would show a corresponding improvement. Unfortunately, her blood work did not match these wonderful improvements. Her kidneys had gotten worse. I dove back into research. I was determined to find a solution for my sweet girl. Eventually, I found an Australian homeopathic vet whom I contacted. The local homeopathic vet had declined taking Tapa back on as an urgent case as he was full. I will not share my response to that. The Australian vet, Diana, was a gem. For just $20, I was given fifteen emails in which to communicate with her. She replied promptly to every email, designed an urgent homeopathic treatment plan and shipped me the remedies. I received the first shipment in early July. More blood work the end of June showed a continuous decline in Tapa's kidneys. Time was running out. She had begun vomiting again towards the end of June after more than six weeks of no vomiting at all. Her nausea was increasing making it difficult to eat even when I could see she was really hungry. She was getting thinner and weaker.

On some days it seemed Tapa was in pain. She would walk as though her hips were hurting, and curl up into a tight little ball to sleep with her legs pulled close to her body. I began rubbing the homeopathic cream, Arnica, into her legs. At night I place a warm heating pad under the blanket which she seemed to love. I often did small treatments of alternating ice packs and the heating pad over her kidneys, and she would just melt. She was having good days and bad days. On the bad days, I put her on the couch in the living room, played soft music for her or read poems to her, and sometimes just sat and sat with her praying for a miracle. At night we would lay on the bed, and talk. On her good days, she mustered all the strength she had for a walk by the bay or on the beach. Though she would start off full of adrenalin and excitement, it was getting harder and harder for her to exert much energy. My heart was sinking.

Hope for Homeopathy

I began the homeopathic remedies for Tapa knowing this was my last hope, and tried to overcome the fear of it being too late. I stopped all the vet meds both intuitively, and upon the advice of the Aussie vet, Diana. It was her belief that Tapa's kidneys could not recover if they were consistently trying to filter the vet meds. She also confirmed my research that Blue Heelers cannot tolerate meds and drugs like other dogs. I put my faith in this process and prayed a lot.

I began remedies for her kidneys, high blood pressure and nausea. Diana changed Tapa's diet to exclude the rice and yams, and to replace these with squash and pumpkin. It was a full time job giving the remedies at very close intervals throughout the entire day. After 10-12 days I was seeing only minor improvements. She was still battling nausea, periodic vomiting, decreased appetite and lethargy. Diana then did what she called a Bioscan; a long distance intuitive reading on Tapa to see what she needed, and shipped me these remedies. While waiting for these, Tapa developed a bladder infection. Diana put me in touch with a pet store owner in North Carolina who could ship me more remedies quickly to treat this as well as send me remedies for what Diana suspected was also either an ulcer, gastritis or pancreatitis...all common ailments related to kidney disease. It was this woman, also another Diana, who said it was imperative Tapa was being treated with a probiotic and enzymes, which I had not done. She reminded me the antibiotic doxycycline had probably killed all her good bacteria along with the bad, and disrupted her enzyme production. Both of these would be contributing to her vomiting. My heart sank that I had overlooked these vital additions. After only two days on these, Tapa's vomiting lessened and her appetite improved. She would eat a little something now during the day, and make an effort to eat dinner.

Upon instructions from the vet Diana, I was to administer each remedy separately now, watch for results and then focus just on those remedies to which Tapa responded. After four days, I was to repeat the process, and continue to monitor the remedies which gave immediate results. Her bladder infection cleared, and I could sense her gut had calmed down considerably. But she was so thin. In just a matter of a week she had lost so much muscle mass. I was praying the pro-biotic and enzymes would heal her gut sufficiently to increase her appetite back to normal. It never happened. She began vomiting regularly in the wee hours of the morning, and re-fused to eat or drink all day. She did not show any interest in play-ing anymore nor taking walks. I began to see sadness in her eyes, and I would find her curled up in a corner somewhere. It was now the end of July, and five months of battling her illness. The vet had told me that six months was all she would have if her kidneys did not bounce back. I went to see him, to have the dreaded talk. We both agreed Tapa no longer had kidney disease, but kidney failure. He said seizures would start to come next. I could not watch her endure seizures nor continue this slow death. I asked him if he could come to my house five days later, to help me put an end to her suffering. It was time to let her go.

Letting Go

The next five days were both brutal and special. I, of course, went back and forth with my decision mentally, though my heart knew it was time. It was excruciating. I questioned if I was doing the right thing, doubted if I had done all I could or done it right. But then I would look at her, so thin and sad, and I could no longer deny she had lost the quality of life she loved. She knew she was dying. She needed me to be strong to help her go. It took everything I had left.

I took her to the ocean's edge where we just laid on a blanket listening to the sound of the waves. At home, we laid on the grass in the shade beneath fragrant flowering trees, and just watched life. I rubbed her belly and her soft, black velvet ears a zillion times. I read her poems by Mary Oliver. I let her eat whatever she wanted

when she wanted. I never left her side, and tried not to cry. I wrote her a farewell poem. I took the last photos. I could not imagine my life without her.

On Friday August 9th at 6:30 pm, the vet came to my house. My son and a girlfriend were there for support. I lit the four candles in front of her photos, burned sweetgrass incense and together Tapa and I laid on a pile of blankets on my studio floor. The vet lightly sedated her while my son James read my poem beneath his tears. When he was done, the vet administered the med to send her on her way. She left very quickly. I was holding her close, and could feel the moment her sweet soul took flight like a winged bird. I felt a part of me go with her...forever.

I laid there on the blankets with my body wrapped close around her and cried an ocean of tears. I did not know how I would go on without my sweet Tapa. Though I felt the relief of her suffering finally over, I sensed more a painful rip in my being—a giant chasm of finality that my heart could not accept. I was exhausted. My son carried her body's empty shell to the vet's car where he laid on her on a sheepskin pad. I stood in the driveway, and watched his car disappear out of sight with yet another chapter of my life closed.

Leptospirosis

What is Leptospirosis?

Leptospirosis is a disease caused by spiral bacteria called spirochetes or leptospires. Two spirochetes have adapted to cause disease in dogs: the Borrelia which causes Lyme disease and Leptospira which results in Leptospirosis. Of the 230 identified strains of Leptospirosis, eight of them are responsible for disease in dogs, though the Lepto tests only list six of these strains. Lepto occurs worldwide, but seems to be most prevalent in mild or tropical climates with heavy rainfall. It will not tolerate freezing temperatures. However, I did hear of a case in Wyoming this summer so it is beginning to show up in drier climates during the warmer months. Lepto is perpetuated in wildlife, specifically in raccoons, opossums, skunks, squirrels and rats. These wildlife carriers do not appear sick as their antibodies tend to clear the spirochetes from most of their organs, except the kidneys, where the bacterium persists in the microscopic tubes that carry urine to the bladder. Infected wildlife contaminates the environment with living Lepto bacteria when they urinate. The leptospira, which they shed for months or even years, remains active in water, mud, dampness and more alkaline soils. For this reason, hunting and working dogs that spend time in swampy, wooded areas or swim in still water are most susceptible. Leptospira are often washed by rain into pools of standing water or into lakes. A dog is exposed simply by sniffing the urine, or by drinking or swimming in contaminated water.

Oleta National Park here in Miami is the perfect breeding ground for the leptospira bacteria. It is full of standing water with swampy trails through dense tropical vegetation which offers ideal homes for wildlife. Tapa could have picked up the scent from one of these wild animals who were most likely carriers. She also could have gotten it in my son's or my backyard where raccoons, opossums and rats frequently visit. It is crucial to protect your dog if taking them to these kinds of environments. Lepto is on the rise, and I suspect in time could easily catch up with Lyme. I hope not as it is far worse and more fatal.

Symptoms

It is possible for a dog to be exposed to Lepto, and not become visibly ill right away. The symptoms vary from each dog, and perhaps some dogs have mild exposures in which the accumulated antibodies manage to ward off an acute attack. However, over time, kidney disease could suddenly develop. The exposure time frame in which dogs become sick can be anywhere from 2 to 30 days though 4 to 12 days is more common. The bacterium spreads very rapidly through the blood stream, and produce potent toxins which aggressively attack the organs—especially the kidneys. The extent of the damage will depend upon the various strains, the level of exposure and how quickly the dog is diagnosed and treated.

Typical symptoms tend to be the following:

- Vomiting
- Loss of appetite
- Fever
- Shivering
- Joint and muscle pain
- Stiffness
- Depression
- Lethargy
- Stomach pain
- Increased/decreased thirst
- Diarrhea
- Weakness

These can be the initial symptoms soon after exposure. As the disease progresses, there can be more severe symptoms in relation to the organs it attacks. These can include eye inflammation, temporary blindness, high blood pressure, bladder infections, jaundice, dehydration, vomiting yellow bile, blood clots, appetite loss, ulcers, gastritis, pancreatitis and a total disinterest in drinking water. Since Lepto favors the attack of the kidneys, kidney damage is most common with significant changes in the BUN and Creatinine kidney values. Ongoing blood work will indicate which organs have been hardest hit. The health of the kidneys will be an issue in most every dog with Lepto. Though Tapa's acute attack resulted in multiple organ failure, her liver and pancreas did make a full recovery. Severely damaged kidneys can be temporary or permanent. You will not know the extent of the damage until you have treated and killed the leptospira. Then it becomes a dreadful waiting game.

I strongly suggest you have blood work done immediately upon seeing any of the symptoms listed above. Time is of the essence with Lepto. Your dog's chance of survival is greatly increased by how fast this disease is diagnosed. It takes five to seven days for the Lepto test results so if there is any suspicion of Lepto, do not delay. Tapa went undiagnosed for almost three weeks from the time she started vomiting. The vet suspected Lepto so anti-biotic IV fluids were started before we knew for sure, but a lot of time had passed in which the Lepto was at harmful work. We now know just how much damage can be done in a very short amount of time by these deadly bacteria.

Treatment

Antibiotics, like Doxycycline, will kill the Lepto, and is usually a three week treatment. This early stage is very severe and challenging so your dog needs good, supportive care. Doxycycline is very strong, and consistently flattened Tapa. It is good to include at this stage a quality probiotic, anti-vomiting meds or homeopathic remedies and IV fluids three to five times a week. As far as I know, there is no homeopathic remedy that kills Lepto like antibiotics, though there are Leptospirosis homeopathic nosodes to prevent the disease. You need to know whatever treatment you choose is going to do its job quickly as you want this bacteria dead as fast as possible. If I were to do this over again, I would begin several homeopathic remedies at this stage to help support the kidneys and liver, give some relief from the side effects of the doxy and help detoxify. It took me a few weeks before I began to do this, and I saw an immediate improvement in Tapa when I did. Your dog is going to be feeling very bad at this stage. I often made big pots of chicken broth to which I added some coconut oil, Chia seeds and detox herbs, and brought it to her in a bowl on the couch. She was often too sick to stand up and eat. Sometimes I had to syringe it in her mouth when she did not even want to sit up. The doxy is given twice a day, and you must try to get some food in them beforehand as it is so hard on their stomach. When Tapa turned her nose up to everything, goat yogurt was always a winner.

Vaccines

The vaccine for Lepto has more serious reactions than any other vaccine, some of them fatal. Thus, only vaccinate your dog if you are certain exposure is likely. If you live in a dry climate, and are going to travel with your dog to warm, wet, tropical climates, this vaccine needs to be considered if your dog loves to romp in nature. Many hunting dog owners need to consider this vaccine in the warm weather. The Lepto vaccine is also very short lived, maybe one year or even less, and there are questions regarding how effective it really is. Vaccine manufacturers have yet to perfect this vaccine, and it may be some years before they do. Their job is complicated by the eight strains. If your dog becomes infected by three of these strains, they will remain immune to these specific strains so long as the anti-bodies remain in their body. However, they remain vulnerable to infection from exposure to the other strains for which they have no anti-bodies.

I personally would reconsider traditional veterinary vaccines entirely. I realize this can feel like a scary proposition especially when a dog's risk of exposure is high in some situations. But vaccines are positively overwhelming and shocking to your dog's immune system. According to some recent studies, vaccine reactions are currently at an all time high, and surpassing the vaccine manufacturer's rates for these incidences. Did you know that your six pound Chihuahua gets the same size vaccine as your eighty-five pound Labrador? This clearly explains the more common adverse reactions in small dogs compared to larger dogs, yet no adjustments are being made.

It is vital to know the following facts:

- Studies are beginning to point the finger at vaccines for being the cause of many medical problems related to the immune system in dogs such as anemia, cancer, allergies and seizures.

- Most vets and Big Pharm are conveniently joined at the hip making a lot of money, thus neither of them are willing to challenge nor question the real necessity for these vaccines.

- Some vets who are speaking out are noted for explaining that one annual vaccine provides enough immunity to last for many years, and there is no evidence to the contrary.

- All the many vaccines suggested by vets are purely recommendations without any evidence.

- Your dog's vaccines contain aluminum and mercury which are hazardous to immune function.

It is also noted that well over 60 percent of all canine veterinary visits are for vaccines. Further, if just the required Rabies vaccine was eliminated for dogs, a small vet's income would drop by more than half. The question then arises as to how many recurring vet visits your dog needs as a result of vaccine reactions and other problems? Veterinary vaccine sales are a $6 billion dollar industry with over $900 million in the USA alone.

Studies being done reveal that many core vaccinations provide immunity for up to seven years. As well, there appears to be no increase in disease for dogs being vaccinated every three years instead of annually. Small dogs are most susceptible to adverse vaccine reactions, particularly the Lepto vaccine. If you are on the fence about continuing with annual vaccines, ask your vet for what is called a Titer test; an antibody immunity test which will measure the antibodies present from previous vaccines. There is no point repeating a vaccine if your dog is already protected. This is especially important if you have a sick, weak or elderly dog.

Homeopathic Nosodes

The vaccine alternative available is homeopathic oral nosodes. Refreshingly, these are completely safe with zero side effects or risks of any kind. These animal nosodes also have a far broader healing protection and capability than vaccines. Most homeopathic vets are able to provide these as a replacement for all the core vaccines, including Leptospirosis and Rabies. Your only challenge will be evading the law for the required Rabies vaccine as apparently the Rabies nosode is not recognized as an acceptable alternative. Wonder why? I think we know the answer to that question. Since these types of problems may arise with boarding kennels, dog daycare and international travel (all which demand specific vaccinations), they present the opportunities to take a stand against the dangers of vaccines. You can show proof of immunity with a copy of your Titer test and propel this new understanding forward. It is so unfortunate that the health and well-being of our beloved dogs are being jeopardized by yet another round of corporate greed.

Canine Kidney Disease

Canine kidney disease is classified as either acute or chronic. Chronic kidney disease most often affects older dogs. If your dog becomes infected with Leptospirosis, you will be facing acute kidney disease. The Lepto bacteria aggressively attack a dog's kidneys, and it is usually this acute attack that alerts you to the fact your dog is sick. While chronic kidney disease develops slowly over a long period of time, acute kidney disease as a result of Lepto will cause rapid, irreversible damage to the kidneys. Unfortunately, you and your dog are in for a rough ride with acute kidney disease. It becomes a painful waiting game while you care for your dog and wait to find out what damage has been done—hopefully avoiding renal failure.

You will immediately need to begin IV fluids on a regular basis and decide on using vet meds versus homeopathy remedies. You will also need to adjust or supplement your dog's diet. Check the Resources chapter to find a list of homeopathy remedies which can be used to treat kidney disease. Changes to your dog's diet will include:

- Reducing phosphorous most commonly found in bones, dairy, fish, organ meats and egg yolks.

- Maintain moderate levels of fat to increase caloric intake without increasing phosphorous, such as providing salmon oil, chicken fat, moderate amounts of goat yogurt or eggs, chicken and turkey with the skin, moderate amounts of ground beef.

- Maintain moderate protein levels. Green tripe, raw freeze dried or raw frozen chicken or turkey will work well along with a low protein kibble which can include yams, winter squash or white rice.

- Eliminating all sodium.

Symptoms as a result of acute kidney disease can include high blood pressure, anemia, fluid retention, lethargy, vomiting, depression, blood clotting, appetite loss, nausea, ulcers and gastritis. You will need to be prepared to treat these symptoms as they occur either with your vet or with homeopathy. I have included some good websites in the Resources chapter. You will need to spend some time learning all you can about acute canine kidney disease so as to understand exactly what you are dealing with, and how to help your dog in the best way possible.

The Way of the Vet

I have great respect for veterinarians. They are some of the hardest working, most dedicated people who give their best to help care for our dogs. I am not, however, fond of their affair with Big Pharm. I feel it clouds their vision and capacity for flexibility, change and being open to better options. In some ways, I feel betrayed. Vet meds and drugs seem to be routinely handed out to every dog owner with little discussion of neither their ingredients nor their side effects when we know every dog is likely to have a different response and reaction. Big Pharm has the same agenda with our species, the only difference being we humans can voice how badly a particular drug makes us feel. Who is to say our dogs are not tolerating unpleasant side effects they cannot tell us about. I have no doubt they would tell us if they could.

It is my belief that we humans, our dogs and all sentient beings are intended to live in harmony with nature. A dog will find grass to eat when their stomach is upset. A person will know what foods they might want to eat when not feeling well. The truth is that everything we need to sustain optimal health can be found in the natural world. Modern medicine can attribute many of their magic drugs to the plant kingdom. Unfortunately, many of the natural healing substances have been reproduced chemically which eventually leads to harmful chemical alterations. Big Pharm has gone too far and the underlying greed can no longer be hidden. There are serious dangers involved when this level of greed mutates into its own monster, and needs more and more and more to feed it. Any and all initial good intentions are lost and sacrificed to keep this monster alive.

Disease (dis-ease) means we are not at ease with the amount of toxic overload that continually threatens us and our animals in our food, water, medicine and environment. When we take doses of pharmaceutical drugs as our medicine, we are not only suppressing the symptoms, we are setting the stage for the accumulation of toxins in the body to result in future health problems. This is true for both humans and animals. Our life sustaining bodies were designed to eliminate toxins gently and naturally instead of driving them deeper into the body by the use of more blanket prescribed drugs.

Vets not only rely on drugs, but they are heavily into the drug business that generates over $900 million a year in vaccine sales in this country alone. The cost to take care of your dog today at the vet is insane and inhumane. All of Tapa's vet bills for five months came to a total of $7,163.00 and then some. I did not have pet insurance and I did not have a savings account I could drain. I was struggling financially when Tapa got sick. I was fortunate to have family who helped. I felt as though I was feeding the monster more and more while dealing with extreme levels of added stress in an already stressful situation with my sick dog—my best friend. There is something very wrong with this picture. So many thousands of dog owners are faced with this situation every day. Something has to change.

Because Tapa's illness was acute, sudden and life threatening, I had no choice but to admit her right away to an animal hospital. I was lucky my son here had a good vet close by. I was, of course, willing to do whatever it took to save her life, but I had no idea at the time what I was getting into to financially...for months to come. Once I realized what we were dealing with, and the long road ahead, I knew it was time to consider homeopathy both to assist Tapa's healing and to save my bank account. I worked out an arrangement with the vet to make payments each time I came in, and requested a breakdown of each visit's expenses so I could, while choking, assess if I could afford it. Tapa was so sick that most of what was needed for treatments just had to be done to help her, in spite of the cost. I did not hold back from the vets my challenging financial situation, and upon a few occasions, I was graciously not charged for some of the treatments. Upon a few other occasions, I was backed into a corner to pay the visit in full, or tests would not be sent out. This did not go over well with me as I had already paid thousands of dollars, and my current balance was only a few hundred dollars. It felt like a message of money being more important than the life of my dog. On one of those occasions, I had just made a $150 payment, but it was not enough. I used the word bullshit with the vet, and later got feedback from a family member that I was out of control. That is an easy projection when you are on the outside looking in. For me, the entire expenditure situation was spinning out of control with Big Pharm behind the wheel. I needed a new ride.

It was my hope the local homeopathic vet would be willing to work with me on many levels. One of those was to be in contact with the traditional vets so we could all be on the same page. I had alerted them I would be consulting a homeopathic vet. There was an open response, mixed with some resistance, on both sides. The homeopathic vet was a convert from traditional veterinary medicine. This was good because he was familiar with all the vet meds. He was a gentle man with an unusual approach, but something was amiss. I never felt him jump in 100 percent to help Tapa. He wanted to redo the Lepto test because he was sensing there could be an underlying issue, and wanted to rule that out before he treated her. OK. But he had a copy of her blood work revealing kidney disease regardless of the cause, and it seemed to me he needed to dive in and treat her for that. He gave me remedies to help with vomiting, suggestions on how to get her to eat and drink and advised me on which remedies I had at home to give her when needed. It all felt like basic maintenance instead of serious effort to help her kidneys recover.

Looking back, I feel he had an issue with my traditional vet commitment, and he was not willing to give 100 percent unless I did the same. I probably would have if he had stepped up to the plate, told me he had a treatment plan in which he was confident and what he needed from me. After $600 plus, I began to question whether he really wanted to help Tapa and if he even knew how since I was still waiting for an aggressive, solid treatment plan to help her. I did not understand. I let it slide since Tapa was making improvements on the vet meds though my intuition told me I needed to be doing more. It was also very tough to be making payments now to two vets, and I was not getting clear communication from the homeopathic vet regarding payment options for ongoing treatment. He was expensive. I ultimately contacted him again at the advice of the other vet when Tapa's kidney values were not improving, and asked him for help. He emailed back saying I had dropped the ball, he had been kept out of the loop and he was full caring for urgent cases and had no time for Tapa. That email was followed by another disclosing the name of a homeopathic remedy that was supposed to really help the kidneys I might want to try, but it was probably too late. Wow. I could only wonder why he had not started Tapa on this when I first brought her to him with kidney disease months earlier.

I was so discouraged at this point, but I continued to research homeopathic options. I discovered Diana Moon Hayes, an Australian holistic and homeopathic animal practitioner, whom I wish I had found months earlier. I believe that if I had started Tapa on her remedies in April, Tapa might still be here today. Diana is the owner of *holisticanimalmedicines.com*, and she is a real gem. She is so not about the money, but about real, loving care for your dog. This became so clear when for only $20 I was given 15 emails with her to which she replied promptly and in great detail. There were times, when I could tell with the time difference, she was responding very late at night after a full, busy day in her animal practice. I was impressed. I learned so much from her, but more so, our exchange gave me great comfort to have this very personal one on one with someone who was really there, and wanting to help from across the world. I found it rather ironic the vets in my own backyard felt worlds away compared to her thousands of miles away.

The way of the vet can be frustrating for you, and risky for your dog. If you are not willing to continue with an onslaught of vet meds and drugs that ultimately poison your dog, it is time to consider homeopathy and holistic care—not just to replace vaccines and vet meds, but everything; flea and tick meds, heartworm meds—the whole shebang. The fewer toxins with which you burden your dog, the happier and healthier your dog will be...and probably you, too.

Perhaps one day traditional veterinary medicine will escape the strong hold of Big Pharm, and open to healthier, more natural alternatives. Pharmaceutical drugs may have their place, but the dangers, risks and toxicity of many drugs are often not understood in our pets. The life force in all beings has an innate intelligence to heal itself when it is lovingly and gently guided to do so. Drugs should only be used when absolutely necessary, and as a last resort.

The Way of Homeopathy

What Is Homeopathy?

Even though many people today are not aware of homeopathy as a legitimate form of medicine, it is a highly developed medical science that is being used all around the world. The concept of homeopathy is to treat the patient as a whole rather than just focusing on and treating the disease alone. This approach is radically different from allopathic medicine where just the disease is the focus of treatment. Homeopathy was developed by a German physician, Samuel Hahnemann, who believed the healing of disease was a natural, inevitable occurrence when the whole of the patient was treated. Homeopathy medicines, known as remedies, are given to the patient in small doses which prompt the immune system towards healing and eliminating disease. This non-toxic approach reflects a holistic understanding of disease which embraces the innate intelligence of the body's capacity to heal itself. Modern medicine seeks to suppress disease symptoms as opposed to recognizing the disease is occurring on more levels than just the physical. The whole patient also includes the mental, emotional and spiritual. While allopathic medicine appears to cure disease, it does so at the risk of leaving toxic residue in the body while homeopathy is completely safe and free of toxins.

How Does Homeopathy Work?

The principle underlying the mechanics and science of homeopathy is based on the idea that *"what a substance can cause, it can cure"*. It is known as The Law of Similars, meaning like cures like. Homeopathic remedies are thus medicines consisting of anything that causes various disease symptoms. If I am going to take remedies to heal a bladder infection, the specific remedy I take will include the very substance that can cause this infection. Homeopathic remedies also have different potencies which are based on the number of times it has been shaken and diluted. These higher dilutions are designed to work deeper and longer in the body than the lower dilutions. All remedies are available in both liquid and pill form.

The most challenging and time consuming part of homeopathy is diagnosing symptoms. In allopathic medicine, only the symptoms indicative of the disease are considered whereas in homeopathy, all the symptoms are taken into consideration. This is because each person, even if they are diagnosed with the same disease, will experience varied symptoms. If one has the flu, one person might be hot while another is cold, or one might be coughing while the other is sneezing and so on. Each symptom reveals the uniqueness of how one is responding to the disease.

I remember taking my boys to the homeopathic doctor and the incredible amount of questions he would ask. He was drilling down to identify the specific symptoms, and would not prescribe a remedy until he was quite certain what the specific symptoms revealed. Sometimes he would prescribe more than one remedy in the event the first one was not exact. He would tell me the exact symptoms I should see resolved with the first remedy, and if not, I would then administer the second remedy. He was so good at his diagnosis that I rarely had to use the second remedy. I was always so impressed how quickly my boys recovered. The real brilliance in homeopathy is the ability to discover the uniqueness of each person, or dog, in order to treat them successfully.

The best testimony I can personally give you as to how well homeopathy works is from a trip I took in 2005 to Mali, West Africa. I had spent time researching about the recommended drugs for malaria and typhoid, and I just could not get myself to the pharmacy to fill these prescriptions. These drugs scared me after reading about them. I went instead to the health food store to inquire about a local homeopathic doctor, and incredibly, one had just moved to town. Even more incredibly, he specialized in immunization homeopathy. He was amazing. He started me on a series of remedies to strengthen my immune system, but I never ingested any of them. All I did was sniff them. I arrived in Africa with my malaria and typhoid remedies which again only required me to sniff. I was with a group studying African drumming and dance. At meals everyone brought their malaria and typhoid meds to the table to take. It took some time before someone noticed I did not take these meds. I went to get my remedies, returned to the table, opened the bottles and sniffed them. I said, "This is my malaria and typhoid treatment." There was a stunned silence followed by howls of laughter. No one could believe this is what I was doing. Comments began to roll in amidst snickers as to whether I would survive the trip. I smiled. I had a long history with homeopathy and was confident. Eventually, while everyone else was battling stomach upsets, loss of appetite, headaches, fatigue and diarrhea along with four malaria cases and three typhoid cases, I sailed along fat and happy.

Homeopathy for Dogs

Homeopathy is so well suited for our beloved dog's medical care. It is imperative to understand both humans and dogs only contract diseases when the state of overall health and well being are most susceptible to them. Thus, I will address preventive care and treatments in the next chapter. An extended history of pharmaceutical drugs for medicine is setting the stage for disease in both humans and dogs. These drugs are contrary to and disrupt the integrity of the vital life force and energy upon which all living creatures depend. The symptoms prior to disease are sending us a message that there is a disturbance in this life force. When we heal this disturbance, our whole being returns to health...naturally.

Dogs respond far better to the gentle and safe remedies of homeopathy than to toxic pharmaceutical drugs. Please note that you can administer homeopathic remedies alongside vet meds. Sometimes, as in the case of Tapa, an acute, life threatening infectious disease may require antibiotics initially to save your dog. However, it may help to provide some homeopathic remedies at the same time and after the antibiotic treatments. It is a bit more challenging to diagnose symptoms in dogs since they cannot provide verbally all the details. Thus, it is up to us as dog owners to watch, study and learn the particulars of our dog which makes them unique. In this way, when they become sick, we will be aware of the changes in them. I want to address here the vital importance of having annual blood work done for your dog. Regardless of whether you choose to treat your dog conventionally or homeopathically, this base blood work will reveal any significant changes occurring in your dog for which symptoms may not yet be present. I thank Dr. Goldstein for this knowledge. If I had done this with Tapa, many questions would have been answered that now never will be.

All the homeopathic remedies available on the market to treat humans can be used to treat your dog. If there is no homeopathic vet in your area, check my Resources chapter for books and websites that can provide you with a wealth of information. It will not take you long to learn how to provide homeopathic care for your dog. The most important step is to really get to know your dog: their sleeping, drinking, eating and urinating patterns, levels of energy, temperament and every detail you can notice. You can consult a homeopathic vet when you first start out to help you get a feel of how things work. I assure you the more you come to know your dog, the easier it will be to diagnose their symptoms for the right remedy. And a deeper bond will be made in the process.

As mentioned previously, homeopathic nosodes are available to replace most all core vaccines. You will be doing your dog a great service to administer these over toxic vaccines. Again, the less you burden your dog with drugs, the healthier they will be and the longer they will live. Not to mention how much money you will save!

Preventive Care

I had never heard of Leptospirosis until Tapa was diagnosed. It never occurred to me, upon moving to this tropical climate, that there were deadly bacteria from which I needed to protect her. After she was diagnosed, I asked my dog owner friends here if they had heard of it, and none of them knew what it was. This is one of the reasons I want to put this information out there. How to do we protect our dogs from Lepto if it is not made common knowledge? We need to spread the word to all dog owners about this rising infectious disease, and hope veterinarians everywhere will do the same.

Preventive medicine for humans is now becoming more and more common in our society. We are learning the steps to take to keep our immune systems strong which helps protect us against disease. These steps include eating a healthy, balanced diet, drinking good water, ingesting specific herbs, foods and supplements, adequate exercise and decreasing stress. I believe we can take these same preventive steps with our dogs. I cannot say for sure whether having done this with Tapa would have saved her life, but if I ever get another Heeler, I will adhere to this preventive path. Perhaps if Tapa's immune system had been stronger, she might have won her battle.

Preventive steps we can take to care for our dogs include:

- Feeding our dogs high quality dog food and treats.

- Giving our dogs clean, pure water.

- Supplementing our dog's diet with greens, healthy oils and herbs.

- Strengthening our dog's immune system with periodic cleansing and detox herbs.
- Alternative medical treatment with homeopathy instead of drugs.
- An abundance of exercise and love.

I will go into greater depth about dog food in the next chapter. Far too many dog foods being sold on the market today are not healthy for your dog. Avoid all dog foods with preservatives and artificial ingredients. Many so called "natural" dog foods include fatty acid oils which not only go rancid quickly, but are the wrong oils for your dog. Too many canned dog foods are full of fillers which do not support a healthy dog.

Many of us are conscious of the need to drink pure, clean water yet, we may overlook this for our dog. All city water is tainted with fluoride, chemicals and toxins. Most bottled waters, and even reverse osmosis, are highly acidic. Acidic water does not provide adequate hydration. The structure of acidic water creates clustering effects wherein the cells clump together, and bounce off the cells in need of hydration. Alkaline water, with a pH of 7 or higher, enters the body as star shaped crystals which effectively penetrate the cell walls to flush and hydrate the cells. Some dogs have a tendency to get into bad things: dead animals, animal waste, rotten food and trash. Dogs are designed as natural predators with the capacity to handle loads of bacteria. Their stomachs are highly acidic which kills most everything, and their production of bile acts as a secondary defense. But there is always the chance a bad bacteria will resist their acid and bile defenses. Alkaline water can greatly assist in flushing these bad bacteria from your dog's body. If you are unsure of the water quality you provide for you and your dog, have the water tested. You can test the pH level with simple pH strips found at the pharmacy.

A high quality dog food will include necessary and essential vitamins and minerals, but it does no harm to supplement with more. This is especially important if you are making your own dog food. Adding a tablespoon of powdered greens to your dog's diet will supplement the nutritional value of plant based nutrients found in grasses, seaweeds and sea vegetables. The absorption of synthetic vitamins and minerals is very poor. Dogs, like people, need highly absorbable organic nutrients which can be easily digested. Greens also assist in rebuilding the good intestinal flora that is often depleted by antibiotics, vet meds and poor diet.

Many dogs suffer from an Omega-3 deficiency, and as such, many commercial dog foods are making dry kibble rich in Omega-3 and Omega-6 fatty acids. Buyer beware! Most dry kibble has too much Omega-6 which can irritate your dog's joints and their skin. Do not buy any dog food which contains soy oil, corn oil, safflower oil or sunflower oil as these are too high in Omega-6. The good Omega-3 oil is rendered inefficient if the Omega-6 is too high. A good ratio is 3 parts Omega-6 to 1 part Omega-3. If the label discloses a higher ratio than this, it is not healthy kibble for your dog.

You can supplement your dog's diet with coconut oil, fish oil or chia seeds. Most dogs love the taste of coconut oil which is rich in the good saturated fats, boosts energy and helps flush out bacteria, viruses and fungus. Fish oil, especially salmon oil, can be added to your dog's food. Start out with very small doses to prevent stomach upset, then gradually increase to one teaspoon. There is some concern now about toxicity in fish oil as a result of ocean contamination and harvest methods. If you are concerned about this, opt instead for chia seeds which have a good balance of Omega-3 and Omega-6 along with extra protein and fiber. Soak one tablespoon of chia seeds in water until they are plump, drain the water and add to your dog's food. This plumping of the seeds prepares the seeds to release their high nutritive benefits. They have no taste so most dogs will not even notice their addition to their food. Chia seeds are one of the best foods you can give your dog, and yourself.

There are so many wonderful herbal extracts from which your dog can benefit. You may want to consider buying a book which lists all these herbs and their properties. Adding herbal extracts to your dog's diet can greatly enhance your dog's health, and thus save you money at the vet. Combine herbs with homeopathy, and you might avoid the vet all together.

You can assist your dog with a yearly cleanse using specific herbs. (Dogs get toxic just as humans do from modern living.) A cleanse is designed to clean the blood, liver and kidneys which helps these organs repair, and thus strengthen the immune system. When a dog has either liver or kidney disease, the organ not working properly can severely compromise the other organ. It is thus good to treat both organs, one at a time, to detox and repair while clearing the blood of the circulating toxins which result from and aggravate the disease. Canine kidney disease is a result of toxic overload which the kidneys are no longer able to filter.

Dogs cooped up at home all day, and who spend too much time alone, are more susceptible to kidney disease. Try to find an alternative option if you are working and leaving your dog at home for 8-10 hours a day. There are pet services which can watch your dog, or if possible come to your home during the day to walk and play with them. Exercise is vital for dogs even when they are sick. Ample exercise strengthens a dog's muscles, organs, stomach and intestines while stimulating circulation and the release of positive, healing chemicals. Dogs, like people, benefit from affection and loving care. They are in our life to bring us joy so we do not want to deprive them of doing their job by not spending quality time with them. Well spent time together will make you both happy.

In regards to alternative medical treatments not offered by traditional veterinary medicine, both acupuncture and acutonics are viable options to consider.

There are many homeopathic vets using acupuncture to assist healing in animals. Acupuncture uses needles to open and stimulate the vital acupoints throughout the body, thereby relieving blockages along and around these points to promote natural healing. There is a constant, innate flow of energy in the body designed to boost and maintain health and vitality. If this flow becomes disrupted or stuck, pain and illness can ensue. Acupuncture can remarkably assist in pain relief for dogs as well as stimulate organ and immune function.

Acutonics employs the use of precisely calibrated tuning forks which are applied to acupoints, areas of pain or chakra centers. This healing modality is based on sound vibration to which all the cells in the body respond and resonate. Though acutonics is similar to acupuncture, the tuning forks are noninvasive compared to invasive needles while the vibrational sounds penetrate deep into the subtle energy fields to promote healing. Some say sound vibration healing will become the medicine of the future since everything is energy and frequency. We are only scratching the surface in our understanding of life and ourselves as energy beings, and how vibration can assist us, and our dogs, in treating illness and supporting health. A friend of mine exploring acutonics once used his tuning forks on Tapa whereupon she completely melted, and fell into a deep sleep. If I had to do her illness over again, I would have added acutonics daily as part of her healing process. It may be difficult to find a local acutonics practitioner, but one can order these tuning forks and learn how to use them.

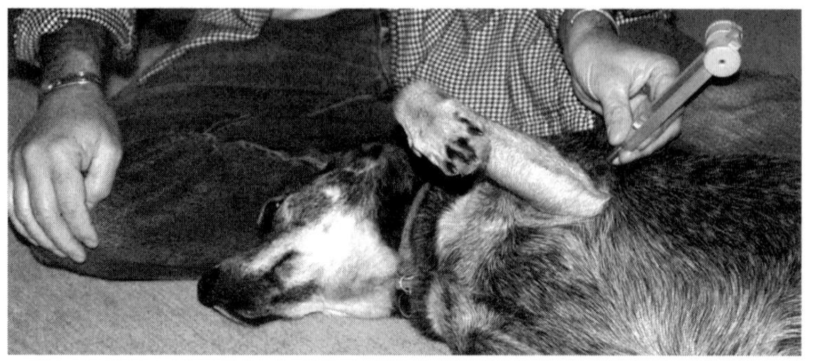

Digging
into
Dog Food

As I mentioned in a previous chapter, there are so many brands of dog foods on the market today, it makes your head spin; organic, grain-free, all natural, high protein, low carbohydrate, raw and more. I hope in this chapter to eliminate some of the confusion, and to clarify your dog's nutritional needs so you can provide your dog with the best, balanced diet. Choosing the right diet for your dog can be complicated by other factors if:

- your dog has allergies

- your dog has a disease or other health issues

- your dog is elderly

- your dog is a picky eater

If any of these factors are an issue, it would be wise to consult your vet for advice on diet changes to provide the proper support for these concerns. However, I will lay the foundation here for a good diet which can be adjusted to suit these issues. Apart from these concerns, every dog is different and will reveal to you their diet and taste preferences. Some dogs will prefer raw meat while others prefer cooked, some will prefer more liquid, more crunch and some will turn their noses up to added oils or veggies. All of these taste preferences can be resolved and adjusted over time once you have the basics of a healthy diet.

Let us start in looking at what makes for a bad dog food and diet, and thus, which commercial dog foods you want to avoid.

Dog Foods to Avoid

No matter how well a dog food is marketed, how unique and cool it is packaged, if it contains any of the ingredients below, do not buy it.

Preservatives

These include BHA, BHT, ethoxyquin (used in pesticides!), propylene glycol (a cousin to anti-freeze!) and propyl gallate. These are toxic, harmful chemicals connected to liver and kidney disease along with other serious medical issues in dogs.

Fillers

These are non-nutritional additives being passed off as protein and fiber sources. They include soy, soybean meal, wheat, wheatgerm meal, wheat gluten, corn, corn meal, corn gluten, ground corn, corn cobs, seed hulls, citrus pulp and beet pulp. Soy is linked to allergies in dogs. Corn and wheat are too rich in sugar. Beet pulp is being used in some high quality, natural dog foods as a good source of fiber but it has been linked to intestinal blockages.

Animal By-Products

There is neither regulation nor disclosure control required regarding the addition of animal by-products to dog foods. These by-products vary, and include the leftover parts of animals: heads, necks, feet, intestines, lungs, liver, spleen, bones, animal fat and more. Most of these rarely include any significant meat. The worst fact is these by-products can be taken from any type of animal in any condition including euthanized and slaughtered animals. Yuck! Avoid all by-products as you have no idea what you are getting.

Unhealthy Oils

I touched on this previously; but again, do not buy any dog food that includes corn oil, soy oil or even small amounts of sunflower or safflower oil. Many dog food brands claim they are an "excellent source of Omega-3 & 6", but the Omega-6 levels are almost always too high which aggravates your dog's joints and skin. Read the label to find a proper ratio of Omega fatty acids with 3 parts Omega-6 to 1 part Omega-3.

Food Coloring

Incredibly, food coloring is still being used in some dog foods, and has been linked to a variety of canine medical issues.

The Ideal Dog Diet

An understanding of what the ideal dog diet looks like will significantly help us choose the right dog food, or create balanced homemade food for our dog. To do this, let us consider a bit of history about dogs.

As it is most commonly believed, dogs evolved from wolves some 15,000 years ago. From this ancestral lineage, dogs are considered to be primarily carnivores in their descent from meat eating wolves. Eventually, dogs were domesticated and evolved in the constant companionship of man, and their survival became dependent upon the leftovers and food scraps from man as opposed to carnivorous kills in the wild. Though this fact indicates a more diverse omnivore diet for dogs, there is a notable and irrefutable carnivorous preference in dogs. Dogs are scavengers by nature, and while they may eat just about anything they find, their diets require high levels of meat protein for them to thrive.

Commercial dog food manufacturers are banking on this resilient, diverse diet of dogs with the production of dry dog food that is primarily grain based and high in carbohydrates. More obvious reasons for the creation of dog kibble is the cheaper cost, the longer shelf life, the abundance of available carbohydrates and the convenience to consumers. Also, many canned dog foods include carbohydrate fillers such as rice and potatoes instead of pure meat content. Dogs, in fact, require very little carbohydrates, if at all, with the exception of extremely hard working dogs. Yet, carbohydrates have now become the main ingredient in most dry dog kibble. If we were to compare the natural ancestral diet of dogs to our modern day dry dog food, we would see something like this:

Ancestral Diet Foods	Conventional Dry
56% Protein	18-32% Protein
25-30% Fat	8-22% Fat
14% Carbs	46-74% Carbs

Dry dog food is so much higher in carbohydrates while drastically lower in protein and fat. Dogs fed these types of grain-based processed dog kibbles will most certainly develop health issues over time. Inflammation is the most common medical response to these diets of higher carbs, lower protein and fats. Another ancestral diet ratio is 49% protein, 44% fat and 6% carbs. You can see how far off we are in feeding too much kibble to our dogs.

Dogs are designed to eat living foods that are unprocessed, raw and nourishing. The best foods are fresh raw, frozen raw, dehydrated, canned and then a high protein dry dog food. A natural, healthy dog diet includes high levels of meat protein, fats, water and minimal carbs. A lifetime of dry dog food does not provide the needed water or protein to maintain your dog's health. If you choose to feed kibble to your dog, look for one that is lower in carbs, high in protein, grain free and use kibble as only 15-20 percent of your dog's daily diet.

Your best choice in feeding your dog is a raw food diet which is fresh, living food, moisture rich and grain free. Though a raw food dog diet probably resulted from trying to simulate what a dog would eat in the wild, we have to be mindful that domesticated dogs have evolved beyond their original wildness. In fact, domesticated dogs tend to live longer than dogs in the wild. We are not trying to return dogs to their wild state with a raw food diet, but increase their health with the nutrients and enzymes found in raw food. I fed Tapa raw food more like a treat, because it was not always her preference. If you choose to convert your dog to a total raw food diet, do your research in order to do it right as changes to a dog's diet can create health problems like pancreatitis.

I am an advocate of raw food which provides essential enzymes from live food, and simulates a dog's ancestral diet. I believe the addition of raw food will increase the overall health and longevity of your dog. These are higher in fat so it is important to start slowly, and raw may not be suitable to older dogs with health concerns. You can alternate between fresh raw, freeze or air dried and raw frozen. You can feed these separately, or mix them in with dehydrated, kibble, canned or home cooked food. Dehydrated is preferable to kibble, but if you choose kibble, be sure it is high in protein and lower in carbs as well as grain free. Not all dogs will like the fresh raw or raw frozen, but most will enjoy the freeze or air dried. If not, there are quality canned dog foods as well as your own home cooked foods. A grain free diet is best for your dog.

There are numerous companies, such as *Stella* and *Chewy's*, who are making high quality frozen raw dog food. You will most likely not find these at the mega pet stores, but at smaller pet shops. *Stella* makes frozen raw patties in chicken, beef and duck which are thawed in 20 minutes, or simply thaw them in the fridge overnight. These are pure raw meat your dog will love. If not, your next options are dehydrated or canned foods. There are two kinds of dehydrated: one is slowly dehydrated under low warm temperatures while the other is air dried. Most of the slowly dehydrated foods are reconstituted with water which provides the essential moisture for dogs. Both *Honest Kitchen* and *Sojos* make these dehydrated dog foods. They are very complete foods which you can prepare in large batches to keep in the fridge. They are also ideal for traveling with your dog since they take up less space and are lighter than big bags of kibble and cans. *ZiwiPeak* makes an air dried venison which can be added to quality kibble or to one of these dehydrated brands.

The quality of canned dog food has greatly increased if you opt for these. *Wellness* makes canned food that is 95 percent meat while *Merrick* makes a great variety of homemade canned dinners. Tapa loved these when she was sick, and they provided the abundance of moisture she needed. I used some of the air dried food as treats for her. I used to feed her *Sojos* which she loved, but she had a tendency to get too thin on this food. It was easily remedied with a half cup addition of either kibble or extra protein. Dehydrated and air dried dog food has the same convenience as kibble, yet when reconstituted becomes infinitely healthier than most any kibble on the market.

To sum up the ideal dog food, and what to look for, choose a brand that is:

- High in meat based protein
- Low in carbohydrates
- High in healthy, natural fats
- A good balanced ratio of Omega fatty acids
- Complete in essential vitamins and minerals
- Free of preservatives, unhealthy oils, fillers and by-products

Read dog food labels so you know what you are buying. Though dogs have evolved to slightly more omnivore diets from their strictly carnivore wolf ancestors, their ancestral diet of high protein and fats with less carbohydrates is still a good plan to follow for their optimal health. If you feed your dog a commercial dry food complete in necessary vitamins and minerals, there is no need to add more of these. This is necessary only if you are making home-made dog food. I do, however, recommend the addition of a quality probiotic to help maintain good gut flora, especially following antibiotic treatment. Also, you may want to add a quality digestive enzyme to assist your dog in maximizing the nutritive value of their food. Other options can include small teaspoons of doggie greens, coconut oil, chia seeds and ground flaxseeds.

There is so much controversy about whether to mix raw food with kibble. It's kind of like eating sashimi with rice when you go out to eat sushi. Some dog owners say mixing the two will give your dog gas while others say it works just fine. It is going to depend upon both what you believe and what your dog has to say. I personally feel it is probably easier on your dog's digestion to keep them separate, and while it may not be a problem in the beginning, it could become one. Feed fresh raw or raw frozen separately as one meal, then the second meal with either raw frozen or freeze dried mixed with dehydrated, such as *Sojos* or *Honest Kitchen*, or if you must, with a quality kibble. Tapa loved kibble so I always tried to fit it in somewhere. I just kept it under 20% of her daily diet. A top pet store owner here in Miami feeds her dogs a quality kibble topped with *ZiwiPeak* twice a day with raw as treats. There are lots of ways to combine fresh raw, raw frozen, freeze dried, dehydrated, kibble, canned and home cooked. Take the time for some trial and error to see what works best for you and your dog. Some dog owners keep alternating different mixes. This again depends on your dog. Tapa did not want a lot of variety in the basics. She tended to stomach upsets with too much variety in her diet. Find what works, then keep it simple. Use variety for treats over too much variety in their basic meals.

In the end, the ideal and best dog food diet is an individual dog matter. No two dogs are alike, and no two dog owners will feed their dogs in the same manner. Active dogs require more carbohydrates than sedentary dogs. Some dogs will love raw food while other will prefer cooked, canned or dehydrated. Take your time, listen to your dog and let him/her help you decide what works best based on their own individual taste and needs.

Homemade Dog Diets

Many dog owners today are choosing to make their dog's food at home. The disadvantages of this are the increased costs, the extra time cooking and the risk of not supporting all the proper, balanced nutrients. The advantages are the ability to adjust nutrient ratios to suit your dog's needs, to know exactly what is in the food your dog eats and the overall health benefits of fresh homemade food.

Protein

If you choose to feed your dog a homemade raw diet, you can freeze your meats for about three days prior to feeding to kill potential parasites, but freezing does not always kill bacteria. Only cooking can do that so if you want to feed raw, be sure to buy high quality meats. Dogs who do not take to raw food will usually love cooked beef, chicken, liver, lamb, turkey or fish. Minimize salt and seasoning when you cook for your dog. Some additions of fresh herbs like parsley and rosemary are fine. Be sure to make some nice broths from remaining meats and bones which can be used to reconstitute dehydrated dog food or added to kibble for extra moisture. Also, 1-2 tablespoons of fat from cooking can be added to your dog's food for flavor.

Acceptable Foods

Suitable foods you can add to your homemade dog food include carrots, peas, broccoli, spinach, green beans, yams, apples, cooked eggs, sardines, pumpkin and squash. Sometimes foods like cucumbers and romaine lettuce can be added when your dog is sick and needs more cooling alkaline moisture in their food. Yogurt, without sweeteners, is a good source of protein, calcium and a pro-biotic. Tapa loved her little bowl of morning goat yogurt. Ground flaxseed can be sprinkled on your dog's food providing a good source of Omega-3 along with fiber. Store flaxseeds in the fridge as they can go rancid. Chia seeds are a super addition to your dog's diet (and your own!) as they have the perfect balance of Omega fatty acids. Brewer's yeast has a tangy taste some dogs love while it provides lots of needed B vitamins. It is essential to give your dog a multi-vitamin or doggie greens if you are making their food to assure their nutritional needs are met.

Healthy Oils

Healthy oils you can add to your dog's diet include olive oil, coconut oil, flaxseed oil, hemp oil, chia oil and salmon or fish oil. Most dogs love coconut oil, and it works great to disguise bad tasting herbs or medicines. Salmon is rich in Omega-3, but it has a strong flavor so start with just a drop or two to get your dog accustomed to the taste. Too much salmon oil too soon can cause stomach upset so go slowly. I read salmon oil is extremely beneficial to a dog's kidneys, and can both protect them and help them rejuvenate.

If you are adding ground flaxseed and chia seeds, you do not need to add the equivalents in oils. Some dogs will clearly have a taste preference in oils, and if not, you can alternate them for variety.

Carbs

Minimize the addition of carbohydrates in your homemade dog food unless you have a very active dog that requires more energy. Healthy carbs for your dog include brown rice, quinoa (always rinse before cooking!), amaranth, yams, potatoes and pumpkin. Oatmeal can be used as an alternative for dogs with allergies, problems with other grains and is beneficial for older dogs.

Canine Kidney Disease Diet

In the unfortunate situation of kidney disease, your dog's diet becomes a crucial factor in helping them cope with this awful illness. Dogs with kidney disease suffer from extreme nausea, lose their appetite and begin to waste away. Though there are special commercial and veterinary dog foods designed for dogs with failing kidneys, the taste is so utterly bland that some dogs will not touch them. The most important thing you can do for your sick dog is to encourage them to keep eating. If they do not eat the bland dog food designed for kidney disease, the best option is to make the most flavorful food possible at home while adhering to the necessary requirements. Your homemade food needs to be somewhat lower in protein (not drastically as some think), sodium free with extra added Omega fatty acids, potassium, calcium and drastically lower in phosphorous. The phosphorous becomes a real challenge since it is found in the protein sources of beef, chicken, fish and dairy. Chicken and turkey tend to be lower so are the preferred protein choices. Cooked eggs are a good choice in moderation. Since the yolks are higher in phosphorous than the egg whites, use one egg yolk to three egg whites. Tapa loved scrambled eggs. You may want to replace rice and potatoes with pumpkin and butternut squash for easier digestion. Add small amounts of doggie greens, chia seeds, ground flaxseed, brewer's yeast and coconut oil to their meal for essential nutrients and flavor. Include a full cup of homemade chicken broth to each meal which will help your dog get the additional fluids to flush the kidneys. You can offer them this broth often between meals as well. As your dog's kidney values hopefully improve, you can increase the protein to normal levels.

If you are unable to make homemade dog food, you can try to increase the flavor of the commercial kidney dog food if your dog finds it bland and uninteresting. A few tablespoons of baked chicken or turkey fat might do it, or added brewer's yeast or butternut squash. Every meal your dog eats with kidney disease is a major victory.

Homemade Dog Recipes

In the *Resources* chapter, I am including a list of good books and websites where you can explore many more homemade dog recipes. Choosing to make your own dog food at home is a personal matter which includes your budget, and your available time for cooking. I had never made any of Tapa's food until she became sick. It was very rewarding to care for her in this way, and to see her happily gobble down something I had made for her. One also learns so much about your dog when you choose to make their food. I have included some recipes for a kidney disease diet because it can be so challenging to know how to adjust your dog's diet to deal with this disease. Dogs with kidney disease struggle with nausea, loss of appetite and many days have a hard time facing food and eating anything. Sometimes I would make three or four different recipes until I found something she would eat. I will address these kidney disease diet concerns in more detail at the end of this chapter.

Raw Dog Food

Ground Beef with Rice, Quinoa or Veggies

Here is a good recipe to prepare in advance and in quantity using raw ground beef which you can mix with either rice, veggies or a mix of both. You can also increase or decrease the proportions to suit how much you want to prepare. This recipe should yield about 20-24 cups.

5 lbs of raw ground beef, preferably natural grass fed beef

9 hard boiled eggs including the eggshells

6-8 cups cooked white rice, or quinoa, or steamed, chopped veggies, or a mix of the rice or quinoa and veggies

5 tsps chia seeds

5 tsps doggie greens

3-5 tbsps of ground flaxseed

3-5 tbsps of coconut oil

Once the eggs have cooled, peel them and smash them in a large bowl. I either use a grinder or the blender to pulverize the eggshells, or you can place them in a plastic bag and roll them with a dough roller. Add the eggshells to the bowl of eggs, add the cooled rice or quinoa or your well chopped veggies which can include carrots, broccoli, green beans, spinach and squash. Add the chia seeds, doggie greens, ground flaxseed, coconut oil and finally the ground beef. I use my hands to really mix all this together. Then I let it sit for 10 minutes so the chia seeds will absorb some moisture and plump up to release their nutrients. Form the raw mixture into patties, place them on a cookie sheet which you will put in the freezer for about 4 hours, then place the frozen patties in either plastic bags or containers to go back into the freezer. Keep out 2-3 days worth of patties, then remove frozen portions to thaw as needed.

To help give you an idea of portions to feed your dog, I found a good chart online. I am also including their steps for how to introduce raw food so as to avoid any stomach upsets. This is important to follow.

Weight of Dog	Amount of Raw Food Daily
10 lbs.	½ cup
20 lbs.	1 cup
40 lbs.	2 cups
60 lbs.	3 cups
80 lbs.	3 ½ - 4 cups

Fast your dog for 24 hours before starting this diet. Water should be available to your dog during the fast. This will give time for the old dog food to pass through your dog's digestive tract. It is vital to follow this procedure to limit digestive upset. This is an important step; ignoring this step greatly increases indigestion for your dog.

Day one & two: Feed a portion 1/4 the size of a normal meal.

Day three & four: Feed a portion 1/2 the size of a normal meal.

Day five & six: Feed a portion 3/4 the size of a normal meal.

Day seven: Feed a full portion.

Special Note: The whole process takes 8 days when you include the 24 hour fast. This method will allow your dog's digestive tract time to adapt to the new raw dog food.

Your dog is likely to have indigestion if you mix this raw food recipe with kibble. Dry kibble digests better as its own separate meal, or mixed with freeze dried, dehydrated, cooked or canned dog food. By feeding raw food separately, your dog will receive the full benefit of its freshness and enzymes. The addition of rice or veggies to this raw mixture will provide sufficient carbs.

Beef Chunks with Yams or Butternut Squash

This is a recipe I would make on the fly for Tapa because she just loved yams and butternut squash. She weighed 35-38 pounds so you can adjust this recipe to suit your dog.

1-1½ cups raw beef cubes cut into bit size chunks

1 cup baked yams or butternut squash

1 tsp ground flaxseed

1 tsp doggie greens

1 tsp chia seeds

1 tbsp coconut oil

½ cup warm homemade beef broth

Put the warm, mashed yams or butternut squash into your dog's food bowl, stir in the ground flaxseed, chia seeds, doggie greens, coconut oil then top with the raw beef chunks and drizzle on the warm beef broth. Let sit for 5 minutes for the chia seeds to plump before feeding your dog. Watch it disappear.

You can substitute raw venison, lamb or chicken livers for the beef. If not doing raw, you can lightly sauté your choice of meat or fish, then add ½ cup of water to the pan to make a broth to pour over the food.

Cooked Dog Food

Tapa loved raw beef, buffalo or lamb over raw chicken or turkey; but she also loved cooked chicken, turkey or beef liver. Usually with the beef liver, I would sauté it in olive or coconut oil, chop it up and add some water to make a gravy. I would then add this to her kibble for dinner. Sometimes I cooked for us both by making baked chicken, baked yams and steamed broccoli. I would mash the yams for her, and top with chopped chicken and broccoli. She loved this meal. Here are a couple of easy cooked recipes I made for both of us.

Turkey Stew

1 pound sliced turkey breasts

2 cups white or brown rice

6 cups water

1 cup chopped veggies

1 tbsp of Braggs Liquid Amino Acids

A few sprigs of fresh rosemary

Chop the sliced turkey breasts into bite size pieces, sauté lightly in olive or coconut oil in a large soup pot, add the rice, water, Braggs and rosemary. Bring to a boil, simmer for 20-30 minutes, add the chopped veggies and simmer 5-10 minutes more. I would place 2 cups in her dog food bowl, add a sprinkle of chia seeds, ground flaxseed and let it cool to warm before feeding her. Then I would doctor my bowl with added spices. She would lap up the broth and inhale the rest before I even had my first bite.

Buffaloaf

I prefer buffalo, or bison, to beef for making meat loaf. I made a buffalo meat loaf one evening. When I sat down to eat, Tapa sat close by staring at me even though she had already eaten her dinner. So I gave her a taste, then another and realized I had a new dish for her. I adjusted the ingredients when I made it again to suit her.

1 ½ – 2 pounds ground buffalo

1 cup rolled oats

2 raw eggs

1 cup grated raw carrots, zucchini and yams

1-2 tbsps Braggs Liquid Amino Acids

A few sprigs of fresh rosemary

Mix all together, press into loaf pan and bake for 45 minutes. This was a great topper for her dehydrated food or kibble.

Dog Treats

The following two recipes for dog treats are courtesy of Diana Moon Hayes at Holistic Animal Medicines. I was struggling to keep weight on Tapa during her illness so Diana suggested I try making dog biscuits. Here are two of her dog biscuit recipes. I made them both, and Tapa seemed to prefer the sweet delights. You can eat this treat yourself if you want.

Sweet Delight Biscuits

1 cup organic coconut flour

1 cup oat bran

1 cup rolled oats

⅛ cup ground sunflower seeds
(I ground them in the blender)

⅛ cup sesame seeds

3 tbsps unprocessed honey

3 tbsps chia seeds

1 cup or more water

Mix all the above ingredients. You can either roll this mixture out and cut squares, or simply shape into a ball and flatten. Bake for almost 2 hours in a 275 degree oven until they are nice and hard.

Herb Biscuits

2 cups of organic coconut flour

¼ cup of dried parsley
(replace with basil if fighting kidney disease)

¼ cup barley grass powder

2 tbsps of garlic powder
(less if your dog has garlic issues)

1 ounce of dried goat milk

¼ cup chia seeds

2 tbsps olive or coconut oil

1 cup water or more

Mix the dry ingredients together then add the oil and water. Knead the dough on a floured cutting board and roll to ¼ inch thick. Let it stand for 20-30 minutes and then cut into squares. Bake in a 375 degree oven until brown. They bake fast, so keep checking them every 3-5 minutes so you do not burn them.

I found these recipes definitely called for more than 1 cup of water. If you overdo the water and the dough gets too sticky, just add some ground flaxseed and roll the dough in a bit of flour until you can roll it out without sticking. If the dough will not cooperate, place it in the fridge to cool it for 15-20 minutes.

These are really yummy, and Tapa loved them. Be sure to bake the sweet delights until they are really, really hard. Store some in the freezer for later use.

Kidney Disease Diet

The right diet for a dog with kidney disease is imperative. Though there are both commercial and veterinary dog foods available for kidney disease, the taste is so bland many dogs will not eat these. You can definitely try to doctor these with more flavors, or have several home recipes you can make. Keeping your dog well fed is a tremendous challenge with this disease. They experience so much nausea which creates a loss of appetite. Think of yourself and how you feel when you have nausea, and how hard it is to find something to eat that appeals to you. You may have to make several recipes before you find one your dog will eat, and even then, this will constantly change. It can become very frustrating, and you will wish more than ever before your dog could talk to you and tell you what he wants to eat. My advice is to have a variety of recipes on hand to help you deal with this situation. Though trying to feed your dog the best recipes for their disease is necessary, it is most important to get them to eat as much as possible. Sometimes this might mean allowing them to eat anything just to keep them eating. You will need to be treating them medicinally for the nausea. Though I am a strong advocate for homeopathy, if it is not working for nausea with your dog, give them whatever vet med will work. It is far more vital at this stage to keep them eating than worrying about the type of nausea treatment. If it works, do it.

Two natural remedies for nausea are apple cider vinegar and powdered ginger root which you can add to their food. The doses for both would be ¼ teaspoon for dogs up to 20 lbs, ½ teaspoon for dogs up to 40 lbs, ¾ teaspoon for dogs up to 60 lbs and 1 teaspoon for dogs up to 80 lbs.

Your goal with a kidney disease dog diet is to provide quality protein, low in phosphorous and highly nutritious with natural vitamins and minerals. It's great if your dog is already eating raw food because the digestion of raw food creates fewer waste products for the kidneys to filter. If your dog is not eating raw food, this is a good time to start introducing very small amounts. Do not mix the raw with kibble or anything else, just small meals with the raw. In fact, you will want to be feeding your sick dog 4-5 small meals a day now instead of the larger 2 meals a day. This again puts less strain on the kidneys.

There is a great deal of controversy about the protein levels for dogs with kidney disease. The by-product wastes of protein digestion are considered to be the main toxins the kidneys need to filter, thus suggesting a lower protein diet for dogs with kidney disease. Yet, there is no real evidence showing that high protein diets damage the kidneys nor that lower protein diets result in significant improvements to renal function. In fact, there seems to be more evidence suggesting dogs with kidney problems actually require slightly more protein to prevent protein deficiency leading to malnutrition. I suggest not worrying too much about this, and just focus on keeping your dog well fed as much as possible.

I was feeding Tapa recipes which included rice and potatoes, but the Australian vet suggested I replace these with pumpkin and butternut squash. I suppose this was because they were easier to digest, yet ironically, they are both higher in potassium. Dogs with advanced kidney disease tend to have high potassium levels. I finally came to the realization that if you simply keep alternating the acceptable foods, you will tend to keep protein and phosphorus amounts at moderate levels.

The bottom line: feed low phosphorous 1/3 protein, low phosphorus 1/3 fat and low phosphorous 1/3 carbs.

The Ancestral diet for a dog with kidney disease is not appropriate now. More carbs need to be fed to keep the overall diet lower in phosphorous. Let's break the bottom line down into a list so you can see clearly the foods from which you can make your homemade recipes. This list will be followed by some recipes all of which you can adjust to suit your own dog if needed. Remember your dog is going to struggle with loss of appetite so you will find yourself constantly adjusting the flavors and food combinations in recipes to keep your dog interested in eating. If your dog goes several days without eating, you are moving into dangerous territory. Do whatever it takes to keep your dog eating something.

Protein

Beef

Chicken with skin – *use more dark meats due to lower phosphorous content*

Turkey with skin

Lamb

Organ meats – *in moderation*

Canned sardines or salmon – *in moderation due to high phosphorous content*

Eggs – *yolks are high in phosphorous, so use one yolk to 2-3 egg whites*

Green Tripe – *contains quality, easily digestible protein with beneficial bacteria*

Fats

Unsalted butter	Meat juices
Coconut oil	Goat yogurt – *in moderation*
Fish and salmon oil	Cottage cheese – *in moderation*
Olive oil	
Chicken fat	

Carbs

White rice	Cream of rice
Sticky rice	Tapioca
Brown rice – *in moderation*	Yams
Barley	Potatoes – *in moderation*

Veggies – carrots, squash, broccoli, spinach, cabbage, green beans

pumpkin, buttenut squash, winter squash – *these 3 in moderation*

Boil or steam veggies to remove phosphorous, but do not feed the cooked broth. Cook rice or veggies in broth or gravy to add more flavor. Try a bit of honey, brewer's yeast or chicken fat if needed to entice your dog to eat.

Supplements

It is important to supplement homemade dog food with essential nutrients. These are the ones I used most often:

- Chia seeds – provides the balanced ratio of Omega-3 and Omega-6 fatty acids

- Ground flaxseed – provides more of the good Omega-3 fatty acid plus fiber for digestion

- Coconut oil – provides healthy fat plus great flavor

- Doggie greens – provides all the essential vitamins, minerals, enzymes and amino acids

- Ground eggshells – provides the extra calcium to bind phosphorous

Recipes for Kidney Disease

Divide these recipes into small servings throughout the day.

Egg and Yams

2 hardboiled eggs

3 cups boiled or baked yams

1 cup small chopped veggies

1 tsp ground eggshells

1 tbsp coconut oil

1 tsp chia seeds

1 tsp ground flaxseed

1 tsp doggie greens

2 tbsps chicken fat or 1 tbsp butter

Rice and Beef

1 cup cooked or raw ground beef

2 cups cooked white rice in beef broth

1 cup small chopped veggies

1 tsp ground eggshells

1 tbsp coconut oil

1 tsp chia seeds

1 tsp ground flaxseed

1 tsp doggie greens

½ cup beef broth (to drizzle over each serving)

Chicken (or Turkey) and Potatoes

1 cup baked chicken thighs or breasts with skin

3 cups boiled white potatoes or yams

1 tsp ground eggshells

1 tbsp coconut oil

1 tsp chia seeds

1 tsp ground flaxseed

1 tsp doggie greens

2 tbsps chicken fat

½ cup chicken broth (to drizzle over each serving)

Brown Rice with Lamb

1 cup raw or cooked, ground or cubed lamb

2 cups cooked brown rice

1 cup small chopped veggies

1 tsp ground eggshells

1 tsp chia seeds

1 tsp ground flaxseed

1 tsp doggie greens

½ cup lamb broth (to drizzle over each serving)

Sticky Rice with Salmon

2 cans pink salmon in water

2 cups cooked sticky rice

2 hardboiled eggs

1 tsp ground eggshells

1 tsp chia seeds

1 tsp ground flaxseed

1 tsp doggie greens

1 tsp coconut oil

2-3 drops salmon oil

Chicken with Barley

1 cup baked chicken thighs or breasts

1 cup cooked white rice

1 cup cooked barley

1 cup small chopped, steamed veggies

1 tsp ground eggshells

1 tsp chia seeds

1 tsp ground flaxseed

1 tsp doggie greens

2 tbsps chicken fat

½ cup chicken broth (to drizzle over each serving)

Final Tips and Suggestions

Since your dog's taste and eating moods will change often, I suggest you prepare some grains and potatoes in advance to have on hand. This will also save you cooking time. You can steam some veggies while you cook your meats.

Cook the meats just before you feed your dog. Your dogs, just like people, enjoy the smell of meat cooking, and this can help excite their appetite

In giving the small, frequent meals, you can do something like this:

- 7-8 am: a small bowl of goat yogurt, cottage cheese or scrambled eggs

- 10-11 am: a small serving of raw meat

- Noon-1 pm: a portion of a cooked recipe

- 3-4 pm: a bowl of chicken or beef broth, some freeze-dried meat or green tripe

- 6-7 pm: a portion of a cooked recipe

- Give the IV fluids at least one hour before feeding.

- Feed your dog something before you give vet meds or homeopathy remedies.

- On days when your dog does not want to eat, offer bowls of broth.

Be sure to give your dog a quality probiotic, as well as digestive enzymes which can be sprinkled on their food, yogurt, and cottage cheese or given separately in a syringe when mixed with water.

To heal ulcers or gastritis common to canine kidney disease, mix Slippery Elm powder with warm water, let it sit until it gels, then add to food or administer in a syringe. Slippery Elm is pure magic and will heal ulcers and gastritis in a matter of a few days.

Coping With Loss

As dog owners we all share in both the life and the death of our beloved dog friends. While our days are filled with the splendid joy they bring us, the inevitable day will come when our dogs must leave us. There is just no easy passing of our sweet companions, whether it is an unexpected or sudden passing, a natural passage or the most unwanted decision to help them pass in putting them to sleep. In many ways, I feel the latter is the most difficult as it leaves us prone to questioning and doubting if we have done the right thing. Though our dogs will usually tell us when they are ready to go, it remains a heart wrenching choice.

The loss of a dog to canine kidney failure is especially painful. It is agonizing to watch your once happy, healthy dog begin to waste away while you try everything within your power to help them heal, and save their life. I felt a part of me was slowly dying with Tapa, and her battle became my battle. It takes so much strength and courage to stay on the bright side as you both cope with depression and grief. Yet, there was a small gem glowing in the darkness which afforded me the chance to become ever more present with my love for her, and to prepare myself for her loss. Even with a belief that all life is eternal, that death is a transformation in which the spirit lives on, that nothing is ever wasted nor truly dies, it remains hard to let go. Coping with loss is both a test and a testimony of our capacity to flow with the natural rhythms of life.

As with all loss of those we love, a time of grieving is necessary and natural. I work at home so I dreaded staying in the quiet of the house where I would often find myself looking for her in all the places she once occupied. I dreaded even more going out and returning to an empty house where I promptly collapsed in tears on the couch in the absence of my usual warm greeting. The grief process is very personal and varies for each person. For myself, I prayed time would go by as quickly as possible. I allowed myself to cry and cry hoping this river of tears would eventually cleanse me of my pain. I was quite shocked at the size of this tearful river that flowed which made me realize the depth of my bond and love for this dog. It was clear I needed to do something creative to honor her, and to help me make peace. I also came to the realization how utterly exhausted I was after our five month battle. I took time off to rest, swim in the ocean, feel my feelings and reflect on the last seven years with Tapa.

I moved through all the stages of grief and loss: shock and denial, anger, guilt and depression with an attempt at acceptance and recovery. I was shocked every time I realized Tapa was gone. I would look at her photos and ashes, and shake my head in denial of her illness and her death. I punched pillows in anger, and then grieved with guilt. Could I have prevented her illness? What did I do wrong? Did I do enough? Did I do her justice in putting her down? I was angry she had been taken away from me, and steeped in feeling responsible. It is a vicious cycle that fortunately has an end.

The hardest part for me was depression. As I reflected on all my years with Tapa, I thought mostly of all the joy and laughter she brought to me every day that now was gone. Gone were her sweet notifications it was time for me to put the paint brush down or leave the computer screen for a healthy dose of sunshine with a walk or round of Frisbee; gone was her magic in drawing people and experiences into my life by her unique appearance and personality; gone was her constant, loyal companionship that softened the edges of loneliness. It was a selfish depression, the price I was paying for her unequivocal love.

Numerous studies have been done revealing the impact of pets on owners. Pet owners are shown to have far less illness than non-pet owners, and significantly faster recovery from severe health problems. As well, pet owners who live alone experience far less loneliness while being afforded an advantageous ease in meeting others through their dog. In short, dog owners and their dogs are blessed with happier and healthier lives from having found one another.

As I moved towards acceptance and recovery, I pondered my belief that we are spiritual beings having a human experience while dogs most certainly are spiritual beings having an animal experience. Like we humans, dogs have a purpose. What separates dogs and humans may come down to the difference in self-awareness. In evolutionary terms, dogs are considered to belong to the second dimension while humans are currently evolving through the third dimension of reality. Though this contrast is deemed to be marked by varying degrees of self-awareness, I rarely felt such an apparent distinction in my energetic exchange with Tapa. In fact many times, I felt she demonstrated a higher sensibility. She knew her territory as well as I knew mine; she knew her dog bed as well as I knew my bed; she knew her bones and food bowls as well as I knew my food and china; she knew her body was sick as well as I knew when I was physically sick. She understood the tones in my voice and the words I used as well as the signs of my movements and moods. In terms of vibration and energy, the intelligence of dogs and animals is superior to human language and understanding. Words often do more to complicate matters than to resolve them.

I have reflected often on one of the best lessons Tapa presented me: the confirmation of the vibrational essence to be found in all living beings. In my efforts to commune with her, I was forced to tap into myself as a vibrational being. I became acutely aware that our capacity to communicate with each other depended upon my ability to tune into her frequency with my vibrations, and to speak her vibrational language. Without a doubt, those vibrations spoke of feelings. Tapa had feelings she needed me to understand and acknowledge. When I managed to succeed at this, she radiated more peace. The hardest conversation was when she told me she was tired of fighting this illness. I knew then what I had to do to help her end the struggle. We were both feeling the angst of having to separate.

I came to accept this dog in all her mystery and wonder. There is no doubt in my being that Tapa was a soulful dog with an equal, if not greater, capacity for love and perception than myself, and who would most likely get to heaven before me. She has come to me at night in my dream time on numerous occasions now. Her spirit is alive and well. I am not alone in this understanding. There are many stories and books available which address the afterlife of dogs, and they are quite remarkable. I have seen the many beautiful, peaceful places where Tapa now resides, and shared in her adventurous freedom there. It is said that dogs whose lives are cut short from illness go to these adventuresome wonderlands where they are given the chance to fulfill to their heart's desire the romp and play they missed. Here resides my sweet Tapa.

Her spirit is now a cherished guide for me which comes with amazing and precise communication that I find astounding. Yet, it makes total sense. She knows I am grieving her loss deeply, and struggling. A few days ago, I was sitting on the back patio in the early evening when the most beautiful cat appeared. Tapa was not a cat fan, and had done her job well keeping the neighborhood cats far from our yard. I am not a big cat fan either, but they have often found me when I have been dogless. I have some good cat stories, and this one seems rather special. This white cat, with most unusual black and tan markings and intense green eyes, came right up to me purring as though she had always known me.

I was so taken back by her sweet and fearless demeanor. But then she moved to the edge of the patio and laid down where Tapa always laid, and when she crossed her front legs like Tapa always did, I felt a jolt run through me. I could only sense in that moment that Tapa was sending me this sweet cat, with all her same colors and poses, to fill in the gap, and help ease my pain.

It has been four days now. This cat seems she is here to stay. Though I refuse to get attached, I have named her Pica. I will feed her, and allow her to do her cat thing. She is affectionate, and her antics make me smile. I feel Tapa smiling down on me in my willingness to receive what feels like her gift to help me heal. And while I sense Tapa would do anything to be here so she could chase this cat from her territory, she knows I have a soft spot for animals. Based on watching Pica fiercely chase another cat this evening from the yard, I think Tapa has chosen well.

Pica's presence will keep my heart soft instead of growing hard in grief. I don't think I need to tell Tapa that Pica cannot begin to replace her. But it would be just like Tapa, at least for now, to keep pouring out her no holds barred love for me any way she can, even if it means resorting to a cat to make me smile again.

Resources

Websites

Dog Food

http://truthaboutpetfood.com

Truth About Pet Food is an excellent website which includes recalls, pet food ingredients, pet food regulations, pet food reviews and pet food news. You can find a review here for most all dog foods plus find a lot of in depth info about dog food ingredients. I highly recommend you check in with this site periodically to check for any recalls in the food you feed your dog.

http://dogfoodadvisor.com

The Dog Food Advisor is another top site for dog food reviews and recalls plus they have a forum you can join. He does an excellent job with his dog food reviews which can help you narrow your search for a good dog food.

http://rawdogranch.com

A really nice site by a couple who walk their talk. They have all their dogs eating raw, lots of proof why this is the best diet for dogs and easy to follow steps for switching to raw.

http://rawfeddogs.net

This is without a doubt the most seriously, pure raw food dog site on the web. There are no fancy raw food recipes here…just the raw meat itself with everything from beef brisket to water buffalo ribs.

http://homemadedogfood.com

An excellent site for learning to make your own dog food at home. I got many ideas from this site which includes both raw and cooked recipes, how to make a nice bone stock and all the tools, along with the do's and don'ts, for making homemade dog food.

http://dogaware.com

A popular dog site steeped with great info on your dog's diet, health and many good articles. You will also find very helpful info here about raw food along with cooked diets for your dog. I especially like the section on Keeping It Raw with dog owners sharing their own recipes.

Kidney Disease and Failure

http://groups.yahoo.com/neo/groups/K9KidneyDiet/info

I wish I had found this site in the very beginning, but I only found it at the very end. It would have made a huge difference. If your dog has kidney disease, join this group right away. It is too easy to feel you and your dog are the only ones out there going through this challenging time with kidney disease. It is so helpful to have the support and experience from others who have been there or are there with you. Feeding and caring for your sick dog can wear you down. Let all these experienced dog owners help you and your dog get through this with more peace and understanding.

http://shirleys-wellness-cafe.com

I cannot say enough great things about this site. Shirley addresses animal and human health in such amazing detail, and primarily from a holistic perspective. You will find info here on canine kidney disease, vaccines, homeopathy and so much more. I spend a lot of time on this site researching for my own health as well. She has a very informative Consumer Alert section.

http://dogaware.com/health/kidney.html

http://www.2ndchance.info/kidney.htm

Helpful info on kidney disease in dogs are here at both of the above sites.

Canine Leptospirosis

Here are some links where you can read more on leptospirosis in dogs. Regarding the third link, it is clear there are many issues with the leptospirosis vaccine. First, this disease will most likely kill your dog, like it did Tapa, unless you can afford the expense of hemodialysis. Second, the vaccine has not been developed sufficiently, and it is very harmful to your dog. If you believe your dog needs protection, please consult a homeopathic vet for the Leptospirosis nosodes. It is the best option available.

http://pets.webmd.com/dogs/canine-leptospirosis

http://www.vcahospitals.com/main/pet-health-information/article/animal-health/leptospirosis-in-dogs/833

http://www.dogsnaturallymagazine.com/leptospirosis-vaccine-protection-and-dogs-what-you-need-to-know/

http://vetmedicine.about.com/od/diseasesandconditions/a/CW-Leptospirosis.htm

Homeopathy Remedies

Here is a list of websites where you can purchase homeopathic remedies. Places like Whole Foods and The Vitamin Shoppe carry assorted homeopathic remedies, but you may not be able to find certain ones. Below the list I have included a list of remedies I used to treat some of Tapa's ailments. These are the ones I found that worked better than others. Every dog will be different.

http://homeopathyworks.com/

http://www.boironusa.com/homeopathic-medicines/

http://abchomeopathy.com/

They have a great forum where you can ask questions, seek help and learn so much.

http://ritecare.com/

Homeopathy Remedies for Canine Kidney Disease:

Kidneys

Serum Anguillae (Eel serum)
Arsenicum Album
Nux Vomica
Berberis Vulgaris
Natrum Muriaticum

Vomiting

Ipecac (Ipecacuanha)

Gastritis

Phosphorous
Aconitum Napellus
Nux Vomica

Stomach / Body Pains

Colocynthis
Plumbum Metallicum

Supplements

Herbal Remedies

http://caninekidneyhealth.com

I used these herbal remedies early on to help Tapa detox. I think these are very good and helpful though I do not believe they can necessarily cure a dog with acute kidney disease as the site may lead you to believe. The woman who makes them, Amanda Banting, is very nice and I spoke with her a few times. I would jump on these at the first sign of any kidney, or liver, issues in your dog.

Doggie Greens

I used the doggie greens from Canine Kidney Health.

http://caninekidneyhealth.com

Carnivora also makes a good one, Earth Greens, that includes probiotics in them.

http://www.carnivora.ca/html/featured_products/
supplements_and_health_care/index.cfm

Dog Digestive Enzymes

Mercola makes some of the best enzymes for dogs. You can find these at Amazon or on Dr. Mercola's website at www.mercola.com.

Dog Probiotics

Mercola also makes some of the best probiotics for dogs. You can also find these at Amazon or on Dr. Mercola's website at www.mercola.com.

Canine Colostrum

http://livingstreamhealth.com/products/canine-colostrum-
for-dogs

Books

Dog Food Diets

I recommend you buy a good book about raw dog diets before you start your dog on one. Not all the websites which offer raw dog recipes are providing you with the full scope of essential nutrients that need to be added to homemade dog food. You also need to use your own good common sense regarding any raw recipes that include bones. Too many bones can cause problems for some dogs, and some dogs should have far less bones than other dogs. Learn to know your own dog so you can make adjustments as needed.

I have picked some of the best books out there for raw dog food diets. Each of these books will help you find everything you need to know.

- *Real Food for Healthy Dogs and Cats: Simple Homemade Food* – $24.50

- *Unlocking the Canine Ancestral Diet: Healthier Dog Food The ABC Way* – $12.78

- *K9 Kitchen, Your Dog's Diet: The Truth Behind The Hype* – $20.00

- *The Barf Diet – Raw Feeding For Cats And Dogs Using Evolutionary Principles* – $26.85

- *Going Rawr – for $27 you will get Going Rawr PDF, Holistic Dog treats PDF plus smoothie and vegetarian recipes for you to stay healthy along with your dog.*

Holistic and Homeopathy

The first two books listed here are about homeopathy in general, then the rest relate to dogs. I recommend if you are new to homeopathy to start out with one of the first two books so you are well educated in this field before trying to help your dog. Homeopathy for dogs will make a lot more sense to you once you understand the basic principles, which do not forget, you can apply to your own health.

- *Homeopathy: Beyond Flat Medicine – $9.86*

- *Impossible Cure: The Promise of Homeopathy – $16.04*

- *Holistic Guide for a Healthy Dog – $12.79*

- *Homeopathic Care for Cats And Dogs: Small Doses for Small Animals – $3.13*

- *Veterinarians Guide to Natural Remedies for Dogs: Safe and Effective Alternative Treatments and Healing Techniques from the Nation's Top Holistic Veterinarians – $10.96*

- *The Complete Herbal Handbook for the Dog and Cat – $13.47*

Homeopathic Vets

I can only recommend one homeopathic and holistic vet at the moment, who is Diana Moon Hayes in Australia. Hopefully, you will be able to find one in your local area. If not, Diana is willing to work with anyone. It is not ideal to have her be so far away, but she can make some very good recommendations in the event you do not have the option of a local holistic vet. A Google search for either holistic or homeopathy veterinarians will help you find someone in your local area.

http://HolisticAnimalMedicines.com

Another Diana owns a pet store in Charlotte, NC called Pawtique, from whom I ordered some products for Tapa. I was so impressed with her knowledge. It looks like they are building a website at pawtiquepets.com, but it is not up yet. A brief review I found about the store says: *"Pawtique is a holistic pet shoppe committed to providing the latest resources of the highest quality for healthy nutrition, supplements and accessories for our canine and feline companions. The holistic approach of supporting body, mind and spirit is our focus for bringing information and products to our pet guardians."*

Their phone is (704) 544-9515. If you need some seriously good advice, call Diana there. Be prepared to wait on the phone or for a return call as she is very busy, but it is well worth the wait.

The Last Battle

The Last Battle

If it should be that I grow frail and weak
And pain should keep me from my sleep,
Then will you do what must be done,
For this—the last battle—can't be won.
You will be sad I understand,
But don't let grief then stay your hand,
For on this day, more than the rest,
Your love and friendship must stand the test.
We have had so many happy years,
You wouldn't want me to suffer so.
When the time comes, please, let me go.
Take me to where to my needs they'll tend,
Only, stay with me till the end
And hold me firm and speak to me
Until my eyes no longer see.
I know in time you will agree
It is a kindness you do to me.
Although my tail its last has waved,
From pain and suffering I have been saved.
Don't grieve that it must be you
Who has to decide this thing to do;
We've been so close—we two—these years,
Don't let your heart hold any tears.

— Unknown

About The Author

Annie Horkan grew up on a large farm nestled in the foothills of the Blue Ridge Mountains of Virginia, and graduated from the University of Virginia with a B.A. in Fine Art. She is a prolific artist of colorful, illuminating paintings as well as hand-painted canvas rugs called floorcloths. As an artist, she has owned and run three galleries, exhibited in numerous one woman and group shows nationally and internationally and her artwork has been published in various well-known magazines and books. Her artwork can be viewed at StudioBlissArt.com and Floorcloths.com.

Besides being an artist, writer and dog lover, Horkan is a strong advocate for the environment, and humanity's sentient awareness as a means to heal ourselves and our planet. Her forthcoming book, *Shells From The Mountain, A Journey Around the Mandala of Life*, weaves her sensitive insights through stories and travel adventures into a meaningful tapestry. After living for sixteen years in the high desert of New Mexico, Horkan currently resides in Miami, Florida.

The author also invites you to visit the website, **BlueHeelerDog. org**, built in honor of Tapa where you can share photos and stories of you own Blue Heeler dog, as well as join her Blue Heelers Facebook Fan Page at **https://www.facebook.com/pages/Blue-Heelers/ 293871963965738.**

The author can be contacted at **anniehorkan@gmail.com.**